This Book
Belongs to

_____

_____

# on the porch with
# ALDA ELLIS
*(and Maggie)*

Alda Ellis is founder and CEO of Alda's Forever, the wholesale gift and home accessory company she co-owns with her husband, William "Buddy" Ellis. Alda's success in the gift industry actually began with her desire to be a stay-at-home mom. When Alda resigned from her job as a dental hygienist, she began working in her kitchen to develop a technique to permanently adhere paper designs to bars of soap. To this popular line of gift soaps, Alda has added candles, silver for home décor, gourmet foods, stationery, and a personal care product line. Today, Alda's Forever includes three wholesale showrooms in Dallas, Chicago, and Atlanta.

# A Lady with a Gift for Sharing

Besides being a busy CEO, Alda is also an author, speaker, designer, and television personality. She hosts *Sentimental Living*, a television program based on her philosophy of hospitality, family, and faith. Alda and her company have also been featured in several national and regional magazines and trade publications.

The fight against breast cancer is another subject dear to Alda's heart. Alda lost her mother to the illness, and Alda has fought her own battle against the disease. Her first trade book, *Beyond Breast Cancer*, was written to share stories of hope and courage from breast cancer survivors. Through the sale of her company's Friendship for the Cure Friendship Ball, Pearl of Promise Pin, and other pink ribbon items, Alda has been able to make generous contributions to the Susan G. Komen Foundation Arkansas Affiliate.

Alda's historic 1918 home on Red Oak Hill in Little Rock, Arkansas serves as the film location for her television show. To relax, Alda enjoys entertaining, collecting vintage papers, and gardening. She spends as much time as possible with her husband and two sons, as well as her dogs and horses.

## EDITORIAL STAFF

*Vice President and Editor-in-Chief:* Sandra Graham Case. *Executive Director of Publications:* Cheryl Nodine Gunnells. *Special Projects Design Director:* Patti Uhiren. *Senior Director of Publications:* Susan White Sullivan. *Senior Publications Designer:* Dana Vaughn. *Director of Designer Relations:* Debra Nettles. *Publications Director:* Kristine Anderson Mertes. *Director of Retail Marketing:* Stephen Wilson. *Art Operations Director:* Jeff Curtis. *Copy Editor:* Susan McManus Johnson. TECHNICAL — *Technical Editors:* Leslie Schick Gorrell and Jennifer S. Hutchings. *Technical Writer:* Christina Kirkendoll. *Technical Associates:* Sarah J. Green, Joyce Harris, Laura Holyfield, and Lois J. Long. ART — *Art Publications Director:* Rhonda Hodge Shelby. *Art Imaging Director:* Mark Hawkins. *Graphic Artists:* Dayle Carozza, Autumn Hall, Andrea Hazlewood, Stephanie Stephens, and Elaine Wheat. *Imaging Technician:* Mark R. Potter. *Photographer:* Lloyd Litsey. *Photography Stylists:* Cassie Francioni and Karen Smart Hall. *Publishing Systems Administrator:* Becky Riddle. *Publishing Systems Assistants:* Clint Hanson, Josh Hyatt, and John Rose.

## BUSINESS STAFF

*Chief Operating Officer:* Tom Siebenmorgen. *Vice President, Sales and Marketing:* Pam Stebbins. *Director of Sales and Services:* Margaret Reinold. *Vice President, Operations:* Jim Dittrich. *Comptroller, Operations:* Rob Thieme. *Retail Customer Service Manager:* Stan Raynor. *Print Production Manager:* Fred F. Pruss.

Made in the United States of America.

Library of Congress Control Number 2005927024
Hardcover ISBN 1-57486-465-3
Softcover ISBN 1-57486-464-5

10 9 8 7 6 5 4 3 2

sentimental living

*My grandmother used to say* that a front porch is a postcard of all who live beyond the door. As a child, I didn't understand what she meant. It was in later years that I discovered for myself that porches are a symbol of welcoming, an opening of the heart.

A porch, just like any other room of the house, can be made inviting with comfortable furnishings and meaningful keepsakes. This is a decorating style that I call Sentimental Living. It's a style that has nothing to do with money at all — it is simply the personal touch you give to everything in your life, and it almost always includes family heirlooms and plenty of creative ideas.

*Continued on page 6.*

*In keeping with the Sentimental Living style*, I decorate my porch in much the same way as I do my home's interior, where I keep such treasures as a porcelain doorknob from the house where my father was born. My dining room table used to be my grandmother's. And there is a kerosene lamp, now wired for electricity, that was once a wedding gift to my mother. Heirlooms like these are more than just mementos, for our family tradition of togetherness was handed down with them. I've learned what makes my heart happy by bringing heirlooms like these, as well as cozy accessories, onto the porch.

After all, porches have always been a thread in my family tapestry. The cool shelter of the porch gave us a place to escape the heat of Southern summers. I cherish memories of days spent playing games, napping, and daydreaming on the porch. All the greetings and partings of my family and friends also took place on porches. Porch living has its roots deep in the past, but with just a little care, it blooms all the more brightly today.

*Continued on page 8.*

"*My favorite porches are the ones that are cherished for the memories of family gatherings that took place there.*"

*And so, as each new season drapes* the porch columns with purple wisteria or pulls a white shawl of snow around the eaves, I will share this favorite gathering place with you. I believe you will find that Sentimental Living, with its simple decorating ideas, crafts, and recipes, can truly make every part of your house a home.

— *Alda Ellis*

"*Be* **not forgetful** *to entertain strangers; for thereby some have entertained* **angels** *unawares.*"

*Hebrews 13:2*

# Alda meets Patti

When Alda decided to share her philosophy of sentimental living with the world, she knew she would need to find a creative director who could share her vision and help bring this book to fruition. That talented lady is Patti Uhiren (above), a longtime designer of crafts and home décor. Says Alda, "Patti's the most creative person I know! As Project Director, she never ceased to amaze me with her talented way of pulling this all together. Her efforts inspired everyone to do their best."

14

16

# Spring

26

30

32

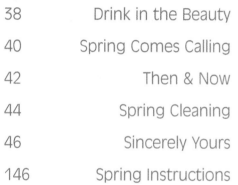

34

36

38

24

40

42

44

46

# Summer

50

58

62

64

66

68

70

72

74

76

56

78

*Autumn*

90

80

94

96

88

98

100

102

104

106

108

110

112

*Winter*

126

130

132

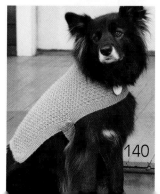

134

136

138

140

142

144

124

sentimental
spring
*a view from the porch*

"A comfortable house is a great source of happiness. It ranks immediately after health and a good conscience," wrote Reverend Sydney Smith in the late 1800's. Even by today's standards, a beautiful porch is still soothing to our souls, and especially so at springtime! Bring your ferns outdoors to thrive on the porch. Freshen your furniture and plump the chairs with pastel pillows for easy Sunday afternoons. There's no mistaking the invitation to your family and friends — "Just drop by!"

# Celebrating a
# Season of Change

Each year, a little Jenny Wren builds her nest in my Boston Fern. In celebration of new beginnings, my family sits on the porch and watches as the wren's dappled eggs become fledglings that leave the nest. This spring, my youngest son is graduating from high school, so our Spring Party holds an extra measure of sentiment for me. Graduation day is not only a milestone for children, but also for parents. Just as the little wren and her fledglings fullfill the cycle of life, I am reminded that I must bid farewell to the past.

The world beyond our front porch is full of choices. May birds, or boys, know that they can always return home to safety and security. The hardest part of being a mother is letting go ...

**The Menu**

**Asparagus
Roll-Ups**

**Shoe-Peg
Corn Salad**

**Ham with
Pineapple Glaze**

**Flowerpot
Cheesecakes**

**Lemonade**

spring

Spring is a time for tea parties, recitals, showers, egg hunts, and graduations. All are wonderful reasons for a party on the porch, but for me, just to see the flowers in bloom is reason enough. The front porch carries with it such grace and charm it can welcome spring and all its pleasures. A cozy corner of the porch might just be the inspiration for a gathering of friends, especially in springtime when the flowers are bursting into bloom. Keep the menu simple yet elegant so that you can also enjoy the party and watch both flowers and friendships bloom.

# Celebrating

# ...the sweetness of Spring

### Lemonade

Always a welcome springtime treat, lemonade may be freshly squeezed or quickly made from a powdered mix. Before serving, add crushed ice and a strawberry or two in each glass and garnish with a sprig of mint.

*Above:* What better way to celebrate the milestones of spring than with a garden-themed party? Large flowerpot saucers make perfect chargers for each place setting. Glue fringe to the short edges of oversized napkins to create quick place mats.
*Left:* For instant napkin ties, simply glue raffia to the back of silk daisies.

# Reserved seating

## Asparagus Roll-Ups

12 slices sandwich bread, crust trimmed off
1/2 cup melted butter
2 cans (16 ounces each) asparagus spears, drained
1 teaspoon seasoned salt
1/2 cup chopped pecans
Parmesan cheese

With pastry brush, brush bread slices with melted butter and place two spears of asparagus on each slice. Sprinkle with seasoned salt and 1 teaspoon chopped pecans. Roll up and secure with a toothpick. Brush top again with melted butter and sprinkle with Parmesan cheese. Place on a cookie sheet under broiler 3-5 minutes until golden brown.

## Shoe-Peg Corn Salad

1 can (11 ounces) shoe-peg corn
1 can (14.5 ounces) French-style green beans
1 can (15 ounces) small green peas
1 jar (2 ounces) chopped pimento
1 cup chopped celery
1 cup finely-chopped green pepper
1/2 cup chopped onion
3/4 cup sugar
1/4 cup salad oil
1/2 cup vinegar

Drain canned vegetables. Mix canned vegetables with fresh vegetables in a 2-quart bowl with a lid that seals tightly. For dressing, heat sugar, oil, and vinegar together until sugar dissolves. Cool dressing mixture and pour over vegetables. Refrigerate overnight to allow flavors to fully mix. This salad keeps for several days in the refrigerator and improves with time.

## Ham with Pineapple Glaze

Mix 1/2 cup brown sugar, 1/4 teaspoon ground cloves, 1/2 cup crushed pineapple, and 2 teaspoons prepared mustard. Spread over baked ham about one hour before end of cooking time. Garnish with pineapple chunks and candied cherries on toothpicks.

Alda finds that nature always provides the best decorations. Embellish your chairbacks with small branches of blooming dogwood, then prepare to hear the "oohs" and "ahhs" begin! Crusty Asparagus Roll-Ups, sweet-and-zesty Shoe-Peg Corn Salad, and mellow Ham with Pineapple Glaze create a spring-fresh menu that complements the season to perfection.

# POTS
## *of*
## plenty

Try using flowerpots in unexpected ways. I have an assortment of terra-cotta flowerpots and saucers that are used exclusively for food. Their shapes make them excellent for use as everything from salad plates to dessert cups, such as when I serve my Flowerpot Cheesecakes. On the porch, they blend well with cut-crystal dishes … and they go through the dishwasher just fine!

## Flowerpot Cheesecakes

6 new 3-inch glazed terra-
   cotta flowerpots,
   thoroughly cleaned
6 vanilla wafers
2 packages instant
   cheesecake mix
   crushed chocolate
   sandwich cookies
   plastic drinking straws
   non-toxic, pesticide-
   free, fresh seasonal
   flowers or artificial
   flowers

*If you're using fresh flowers,
cover the bottom end of your
straw with a piece of tape.*
Place a vanilla wafer in the
bottom of each flowerpot. Fill
each pot to about $1/4$" from the
top with cheesecake mix
made according to package
directions. Place a drinking
straw in the center of each pot
through cheesecake; cut
straw even with top of pot.
Sprinkle the top of the
cheesecake with crushed
cookie crumb "dirt."
Refrigerate until cheesecake is
set. Just before serving, place
a flower in the straw.

**This page:** Clever Flowerpot
Cheesecakes are guaranteed to
win smiles of delight.
**Opposite:** Flowerpots perched
on candlesticks and a gaily
painted birdhouse announce
the arrival of spring.

see

touch      hear      smell      taste

# five SENSES of spring

Just for spring, create an outdoor setting that appeals to all the senses, a place rich with details that will absorb your attention for hours on end. Add a soft timeworn quilt, so smooth to the touch and perfect for an afternoon nap. Plant a lilac tree near the front porch. It will be in bloom on Mother's Day, and the fragrance will linger in the air. Listen carefully for the sounds of birds returning as winter withdraws. The slow creaking of rocking chairs on the front porch gently eases your cares away. And even though the days of spring begin to lengthen, evening lights are still important. Strings of tiny white lights are not just for Christmas. My porch has wisteria trained to go along the eaves of the house, and one Christmas I wove a strand of white lights through the vines. Mother suggested I leave the lights up through spring, so when the wisteria blooms they will be intertwined. I now enjoy the romantic lighting all year long.

*Opposite:* Christmas lights cross the seasons and look magical among Alda's wisteria vines. A timer turns the lights on and off automatically. *This page:* A beloved quilt is soothing to the touch. Spring's warmth causes every bird to sing. The perfume of flowers makes every day special. And iced tea is so delicious, Alda serves it long before summer arrives!

# A SPRING

# WELCOME

May Day is a traditional day of spring celebration. Renew an old tradition of leaving a floral surprise tied to your neighbor's front door. A handful of blossoms put into an unusual container does the trick. Tie up your bouquet in a paper doily, nosegay style. Add a bow and allow enough extra velvet ribbon to tie your bouquet on your neighbor's doorknob. No matter what your age, ring the bell and run!

*Opposite, clockwise from left:* Freshen your own front door with a generous gathering of silk blossoms tucked into a colorful tote bag. A Door Pocket (see page 146) or a white glove will hold a sweet, old-fashioned surprise for a neighbor.

*This page:* To match your tote bag filled with tulips, line up a row of the bright blossoms in orange pails, then place a colorful new rug before the door. The glory of spring deserves a happy greeting, and so do your guests!

*This page:* Want a quick way to capture springtime? Use floral wire to shape real or artificial forsythia branches into a "natural" monogram for your front door. In just a few minutes more, you can dress up your flowerpots with paint, ribbon, and pom-pom fringe.

*Opposite:* Alda's Chalkboard Tray gets out the word — guests and springtime are always welcome! See page 146 to make your own rewritable message board.

# ENDEARING
## INSPIRATION...

*for a* PERSONAL
GREETING

# *spring*
# FRIENDSHIP BASKET

So many people in our lives are special to us. One way to let them know is by offering a simple "thank you" gift for their friendship. It is especially memorable if given for no reason at all — not for a birthday or an anniversary, but just to offer a jar of kindness!

A Friendship Basket, stocked with little Gift Jars and kept by the door, is a thoughtful way to show guests how much you enjoy their company. On page 146, Alda makes these petite jars look extra-special.

*"Fond memories link days gone by with those that are to come."*

*— Alda*

*Raspberry Honey*
3¹/₂  cups raspberry preserves
  7  cups honey
  1  teaspoon cinnamon

Microwave preserves in a microwave-safe bowl on high power (100%) 1 minute or until melted. Stir honey and cinnamon into preserves until well blended. Store in an airtight container in refrigerator.

# An Oasis of Color & Light

or most of us, solitude in our surroundings is not easy to find. However, we can create a place of relaxation just outside our door. As we momentarily step back from the tension of our day-to-day schedules, we can delight in our own oasis of quiet. A cup of tea when we come home after work, and a moment of quietly sitting by candlelight can become our own haven. Even those on a budget can create a place of beauty on the porch, for it is the little things that please our eyes, warm our hearts, and rest our souls.

*Opposite:* Lightweight and lacy, this knit Spring Afghan in robin's egg blue is just right to chase the chill of an early spring evening. Alda's pattern is on page 146.

*This page top:* If your corner of the porch needs a little cheer, then see page 147 to create these no-sew Pillows with jumbo-sized flowers. They're sure to brighten your outlook and your day.

*This page, bottom:* Little scented candles in crystal votive cups, nestled in the centers of silk flowers ... just gazing at this pretty pair, you can almost feel your tension melt away with the wax.

# Spring

Just because you have a chipped bowl, cup, or saucer, it doesn't mean you have to throw it out. Use it on the porch as a plant saucer, a coaster, or perhaps as a decorative accessory. For example, you could add water to a teacup to float a candle — you've just created a place setting for a spring luncheon! These dish ideas are so much fun, you may decide to visit the flea market for more porcelain porch décor.

# ...serves you well

*Opposite:* An old light fixture glows anew when topped by "teacup votives." Use a glue appropriate to glass and metal when affixing your dishes. *Top, left:* Glue photocopied words to the center of a saucer, then encircle with lace trim and buttons. *Center, left:* A clever instant coaster! *Bottom, left:* A refreshing sight ... a floating flower candle in a pretty china cup. *Above:* See page 147 to make a refreshing Teacup Wreath.

*This page:* Alda's very own canvas Chair Covers get the personal touch with pom-pom fringe and a monogram on page 147.

*Opposite, top:* Use the prettiest beads you can find to top your vintage-style Bell Jars. The simple instructions are on page 147.

*Opposite, bottom:* It looks like aged concrete, but this graceful Urn has a secret … see page 147 to discover what a little paint can do.

The French gave us the word "renaissance," which means renewal and rebirth. To me, keeping the past alive by using old things is like creating a little "renaissance." I love using my mother's 1950's rose-printed cotton tablecloth. It once covered her chrome kitchen table, making it a sentimental favorite for me. Yet even plastic chairs can be refreshed with canvas chair covers. They launder beautifully and I keep them ready to be used at a moment's notice. Another "renaissance" idea is creating antique-style cloches using old vases, glass knobs, wire, and beads.

# a *time* of renaissance

"Inside myself is a place where I live all alone and that's where you renew the springs that never dry up," wrote the author Pearl S. Buck. And what better place for solitary inspiration than on the porch? The haven of my porch inspires my creativity. Gardening magazines and catalogs offer ideas for spring plantings, and a large basket easily totes all of the spring publications that I hope to peruse. If we invest in time away from the world of the ordinary and the routine, we receive clarity and a restored sense of balance.

# Drink in the Beauty...

Refreshment for the soul — a daisy topiary in a copper watering can, a Catalog Basket with a handy pocket, and a Fish Fountain that will catch many a smile. On page 147, Alda puts the pocket on the basket and assembles the fountain in a flash ... and that's no fish tale!

and Be Renewed

*This page:* Encircle each place setting with a length of ivy.
*Opposite, top:* Form ivy (real or silk) into a napkin ring and personalize your napkins with iron-on monograms.
*Opposite, bottom:* Ivy vines flow freely from this appealing centerpiece.

# SPRING comes calling

One of the most versatile decorating accessories for spring may be growing in your yard — it's ivy!  The hardy green vines look lush when used to complement a party tablescape.  Even the most inexperienced gardeners can keep an ample supply of ivy on hand.  From neighborly exchanges, I have several varieties growing in and around my yard. You will find that a vintage birdcage filled with flowers and flowing vines of ivy makes a most elegant centerpiece.

Think outside the box to make your outdoor spaces fresh and happy. By repurposing what you already have, some old items can even serve double duty. A suitcase on an old bench is not only a place for your glass of iced tea, it also serves as storage for a book and a light blanket for leisurely moments on the porch. Add some fresh paint and fabric, and "everything old is new again."

then&now

*Opposite:* Need extra space for porch living? Use paint and fabric to infuse an ordinary storage Ottoman with bold color, or renew an elderly valise into a Suitcase End Table. The instructions are on page 148.

*This page:* A Tray Side Table is sweetened with paint, fabric, and trims on page 148.

# spring
# CLEANING

While little birds are feathering their nests, it is also time for us to do a "spring cleaning" of the porch. Tackle the job, from the eaves to the floor, and your outdoor living room will be yours to enjoy for the season. One of my favorite things to do is to give the floor of my porch a fresh coat of paint early in the spring. Later in the summer, the new paint feels smooth and cool to bare feet.

Alda calls this basket of supplies her "spring cleaning" kit. The clean, dry paintbrush is a truly handy tool. Alda uses it to tackle the corners where spiders have lingered, brisking away their calling cards. A paintbrush can also get into the crevices of rockers, wicker, and the slats of the porch swing. With a few quick embellishments, the cleaning kit also makes a thoughtful housewarming gift. Try adding a band of ribbon and a button to the paintbrush, or trimming the top of a pair of rubber gloves into a decorative scallop.

# SINCER

Use modern conveniences to revive a gracious pastime — letter writing! Alda's complete instructions for the elegant Stationery and the pillowcase-covered Album are on page 148.

**ELY**

*yours*

With the invention of e-mail and cell phones, the art of letter writing has become a bit of a luxury. By using beautiful handmade cards embellished with snippets of ribbons, your letter becomes a real gift. Mother's handkerchief sees new use when scanned and printed to create note cards. Vintage embroidered linens are enjoyed time and again by printing them in a reduced size and adding stripes and polka-dotted borders. Keep these papers in a small, flea market drawer lined with photocopies of cards. Then take the drawer onto the porch for inspirational letter writing … or perhaps for those overdue thank you notes!

# sentimental summer

*a view from the porch*

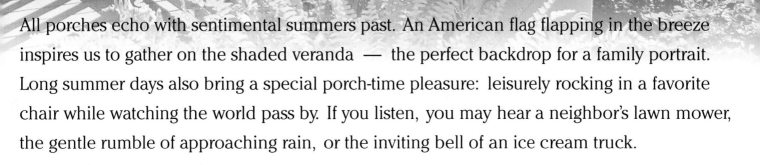

All porches echo with sentimental summers past. An American flag flapping in the breeze inspires us to gather on the shaded veranda — the perfect backdrop for a family portrait. Long summer days also bring a special porch-time pleasure: leisurely rocking in a favorite chair while watching the world pass by. If you listen, you may hear a neighbor's lawn mower, the gentle rumble of approaching rain, or the inviting bell of an ice cream truck.

# the *spirit* of America

President Harry S. Truman was known for his down-to-earth style. He once said, "If you can't stand the heat, get out of the kitchen." Independence Day is the perfect time to take his advice, and move family gatherings out of the kitchen and onto the porch. Once there, celebrate with friends and family over a red-white-and-blue picnic.

The gathering is fun for all ages, and includes lots of sentimental touches for everyone to enjoy. And of course, simple but delicious comfort foods and star-spangled decorations offer the gift of hospitality. A Spirit of America Party can last well into the evening, when delighted *oohs* and *ahhs* greet the colorful fireworks that fill the nighttime sky.

Share a memorable Independence Day on the front porch. See the pages that follow for quick-to-do decorations and Alda's favorite summertime recipes.

*The Menu*

**Dallas Dip**

**Iced Tea Punch**

**Aunt Hattie's Baked Beans**

**Porch Potato Salad**

**Easy Lemon Ice Box Pie**

## Iced Tea Punch

Mix one gallon of iced tea with two cans of frozen fruit punch. Add two cans of water. Serve cold over ice with a garnish of mint.

## Dallas Dip

- 6 large ripe tomatoes, diced and chopped
- 12 green onions, thinly sliced
- 2 cans green chilies
- 2 large cucumbers, peeled, diced, and chopped
- 2 tablespoons garlic salt
- 1/4 cup apple cider vinegar
- 2 tablespoons olive oil

Combine all ingredients and let chill in refrigerator overnight. Serve with tortilla chips.

## Porch Potato Salad

- 8 medium potatoes, unpeeled
- 1 cup finely chopped celery
- 1/2 cup sweet pickle relish
- 1/2 cup small, thinly sliced radishes
- 1 large onion, finely chopped
- 1/2 cup sour cream
- 3/4 cup mayonnaise
- 1 teaspoon celery seed
- 1 tablespoon prepared mustard
- 1/2 teaspoon garlic salt
- 1 1/2 teaspoons salt
  Garnish: 2 hard-boiled eggs, sliced

Cover potatoes with water and cook 20 to 30 minutes until they are fork-tender. Drain and cool; peel and cut into 1/2-inch cubes. Combine potatoes, celery, relish, radishes, and onion. Mix gently with a wooden spoon and set aside. Combine sour cream, mayonnaise, celery seed, mustard, and salts; pour over potatoes and mix, stirring lightly. Garnish with sliced eggs. Cover and refrigerate several hours before serving.

## Aunt Hattie's Baked Beans

- 4 slices bacon
- 1 large yellow onion, finely chopped
- 2 cans (16 ounces each) pork and beans
- 1 tablespoon prepared mustard
- 1/4 cup chile sauce

Cook bacon in an iron skillet until crisp. Remove bacon; crumble. Add onion to drippings; cook until onion is clear. Remove onion from drippings and mix with bacon, beans, mustard, and chile sauce. Brush a 1 1/2-quart baking dish with bacon drippings. Pour bean mixture into baking dish. Bake, uncovered, at 350° for about 45 minutes or until the beans are brown and bubbly.

Summer's heat is eased with Iced Tea Punch, chilled Porch Potato Salad, and mild but flavorful Dallas Dip. Children will declare this Independence Day party "cool" as they nibble on the red-white-and-blue jelly beans scattered on the table.

*Opposite, top to bottom:* Iced Tea Punch, Dallas Dip, Porch Potato Salad, and Aunt Hattie's Baked Beans.
*This page:* Flags and pinwheels fly in bean-filled bottles. A ribbon-wrapped can is an instant planter. Make No-Sew Table Runners with Alda, page 149.

*Each guest is made to feel special as they gather food into their own personal picnic basket.*
*— Alda*

*Easy Lemon Ice Box Pie*
1   quart vanilla ice cream, softened
1   small can of frozen lemonade
       concentrate
2   prepared graham cracker crusts
       Garnish: graham cracker
       crumbs

Fold together ice cream and lemonade concentrate. Pour into pie shells and garnish with cracker crumbs. Place in freezer until firm enough to slice.

For a true slice of Americana, heap ice-cold watermelon into a little red wagon. Line lap-size baskets with handkerchiefs, and let guests add servings of picnic fare. If you will be lounging on the lawn, make old-fashioned "Sit-Upons" from vinyl tablecloth fabric stuffed with newspaper. Alda shows you how on page 149.

Firecracker Favors, with candy inside, team up with a No-Sew Tablecloth to provide explosions of holiday color. Alda shares the how-tos on page 149. For a creamy and refreshing dessert, serve Easy Lemon Ice Box Pie.

hear

touch    see    smell    taste

# five SENSES of summer

To each of our five senses, summer has a distinction all its own. By July, we see hydrangea blossoms that are as big as cabbages. Fireworks sparkle and flags flutter on the warm breeze. Gardenias perfume a summer day and the luscious scent of old-fashioned roses lingers in the evening stillness. Summer is also the time for flavorful, peak-of-the-season foods. Bushel baskets of corn, purple hull peas, tomatoes, green beans, and peaches make their way from the farmer's market to the porch. The shaded space is the perfect setting for an afternoon of shelling, shucking, or peeling the delicious fruits and vegetables. Cool raindrops sprinkle down and we sit out a thunderstorm, watching the drama unfold as a summer rain quenches the lawn. Evening brings the sounds of cricket choirs and bullfrog solos. And children learn their own silly songs to the rhythm of the porch swing, triggering youthful giggles — the most beautiful sound of summer.

*Opposite:* A happy youngster displays the lead singer in Nature's evening chorus. *This page:* A discarded feather is a soft discovery for young fingers. Light showers from a burning sparkler. White pitchers host a fragrant display. And an old-fashioned lunch box holds picnic fare, made all the more enjoyable by the fresh, summer-warmed air.

# a summer

# welcome

My grandmother used to say that a front porch was a postcard of those who lived just beyond the door. As the years have gone by, I've also discovered that my door represents a welcome into my home. To make sure my home is inviting to all who enter, I keep a friendly wreath on the door. And I keep the wreath tidy — wispy little spiders that leave their calling cards are such uninvited guests!

*This page:* Make your guests feel welcome even before they ring the bell. The greeting on this Personalized Plate Wreath is easily updated with a dry-erase marker.

*Opposite:* Any door can benefit from a pretty decoration. This garden shed entry brims with summer joy, courtesy of the Water Hose Wreath.

Alda shares how to shape these warm-weather greeters on pages 149 and 150.

**Opposite page:** An old-fashioned sap bucket holds a spirited display of flowers and American flags. Painting the bucket was so simple! Alda painted it white, applied star stickers, then painted the bucket blue. Peeling off the stickers revealed the shining white stars.

**Left and above:** Alda's father was a skilled carpenter in the days following the second World War. To keep his memory near, Alda places pots of red geraniums in her father's old tool box, a battered treasure that has value beyond words.

**Below:** The yellow dump truck was a favorite toy of Alda's children. These days, the sentimental keepsake has traded loads of rocks and dirt for a cheery potted plant.

*Whether you come to visit,*
*Or just to rest,*
*When you enter our door,*
*May your heart be blessed.*
*— Anonymous*

# *summer* FRIENDSHIP BASKET

It seems that any gathering becomes a more lasting and memorable event if guests are sent home with a special treat. If it is a simple indulgence, such as our Flavored Sugar for iced tea, your guest need never feel obligated to return the favor. Instead, the thoughtful token of friendship will bring to mind the visit long after the day has ended.

Share the sweetness of summer with your guests by treating them to flower-topped bags of Flavored Sugar. On page 150, Alda makes the pretty Gift Bags without any sewing at all!

*Keep a basket of homemade treasures by the door and offer them to visitors as a parting gift.*

*—Alda*

*Flavored Sugar*
- 1   cup sugar
- 1   package (0.23 ounces) unsweetened lemon-, cherry-, or strawberry-flavored soft drink mix

In a medium bowl, combine sugar and soft drink mix. *Yield:* about 1 cup flavored sugar (1 gift).
*To serve:* Stir 2 teaspoons flavored sugar into 6 ounces hot or cold tea.

# refreshing RETREAT

*"Fences make good neighbors, but I think porches make good friends."* — *Alda*

Before the arrival of air conditioning and television, porches were our outdoor living rooms. In those days, we played games outside — jacks, Uncle Wiggly, and paper dolls. You can regain those simpler times in a refreshing retreat made special with pretty fabrics. Share your new surroundings with a friend whose presence is as welcome as the summer breeze, and you'll never miss any of the things that used to keep you indoors.

*Above:* If you are lucky enough to own a porch swing, keep it ever blooming with a Floral Pillow.
*Right:* Whether entertaining friends or enjoying a quiet time alone, settle into a rocker with a Flower Patch Quilt thrown over the arm.
*Opposite:* A flower-printed linen inset adds cottage charm and softness to a Wicker End Table.

Alda's easy instructions for all these blooming beauties begin on page 150.

As the day fades into darkness, cast a warm, candlelit glow on the porch that encourages guests to linger. Candles floating on water are a welcome contrast to the summer's heat, while light from a handmade candle holder makes dinnerware sparkle. When presentation is everything, add candles to your outdoor décor.

"...cast a warm, candlelit glow on the porch

*This page:* Alda's Floating Candles are party-perfect for summer. See page 151 to paint the confetti design. The floating flowers may be the easiest things you'll ever create. Just cut a circle from green craft foam, make a hole in the center, and push a flower stem through the hole.
*Opposite page:* A Hanging Lantern blooms with painted flowers and a Placecard Flowerpot gets plenty of attention. Alda enlightens us with these clever candle holders on page 151.

*that encourages guests to linger...*"

Follow your sense of whimsy to find new vases all around you. For instance, a wicker purse blooms into a wonderful planter.

*Sometimes the smallest containers …
can make a big impression. — Alda*

Actually, it seems my favorite vases are not "vases" at all. For summer's miniature roses, I remembered a favorite purse that went out of style. Now, lined with a plastic bag, the purse is a refreshing "wicker vase." An heirloom silver water pitcher stunningly reflects the colors of abundant hydrangea blooms. Yet any flower in the garden would be charming when so stylishly featured. Gathered on a tray and ready to add romance to a summer tablescape are a child-sized teapot, a stemmed crystal goblet, a sugar bowl, and a porcelain teacup. Sometimes, little containers featuring only a single bloom can make a big impression.

AMAZING VASES

# Porch Living, with

# the *Comforts of Home*

The French call it *élan* — an offhand style that lends charm. Castoffs and old treasures add this quality to a porch, transforming it into an outdoor "room." Two trunks placed side-by-side become a coffee table with the addition of a glass top and matching fabric panels. A small fountain introduces the soothing sound of moving water. Gather up stray magazines and keep them in a cloth-covered basket. If you decorate your porch as you would your home's interior, your outdoor room will become just as inviting as it is useful.

*Opposite:* A glass top and boldly printed fabric give the Storage Trunk Coffee Table renewed energy. It shines as the centerpiece of this cozy porch. A Magazine Basket keeps summertime reading organized.
*This page:* A Multi-Tiered Fountain ensures a tranquil setting for reading, visiting, or just relaxing.

Alda creates all of these outdoor indulgences on pages 151 and 152.

# From garden

*This page:* Watering cans hold bright zinnias and airy greenery. The rose design on the vintage can is an enlarged photocopy of a postcard, glued on and protected with acrylic sealer. Painted in stripes of summertime hues, the Gardener's Mailbox keeps hand tools, gloves, and a kneeling pad high and dry.
*Opposite page:* Wind Chimes made from tarnished silverware will cause visitors to pause and smile. If you love fresh flowers, keep a roomy Straw Tote for gathering blooms from your garden or along a country road. And it's only natural that Gardening Gloves should wear their own faux blossoms. The Water Gun Bin is a treat for mischievous fingers and will quickly be emptied of its contents.

Alda's instructions for these summertime delights begin on page 152.

# delights...

# to water fights...

**and everything in between!** The eloquent writer Henry James declared "summer afternoon" to be the two most beautiful words in the English language. Indeed, these personal touches will bring joy to any porch on a summer day. Welcome friends and family with a vision of flowers in unusual containers and the happy music of handcrafted wind chimes. Treat yourself to a pair of flower-trimmed gardening gloves and a green-striped mailbox in which to store them. And to celebrate a season that's forever young, provide a boxful of water guns and water-filled balloons — great fun for anyone who's willing to run!

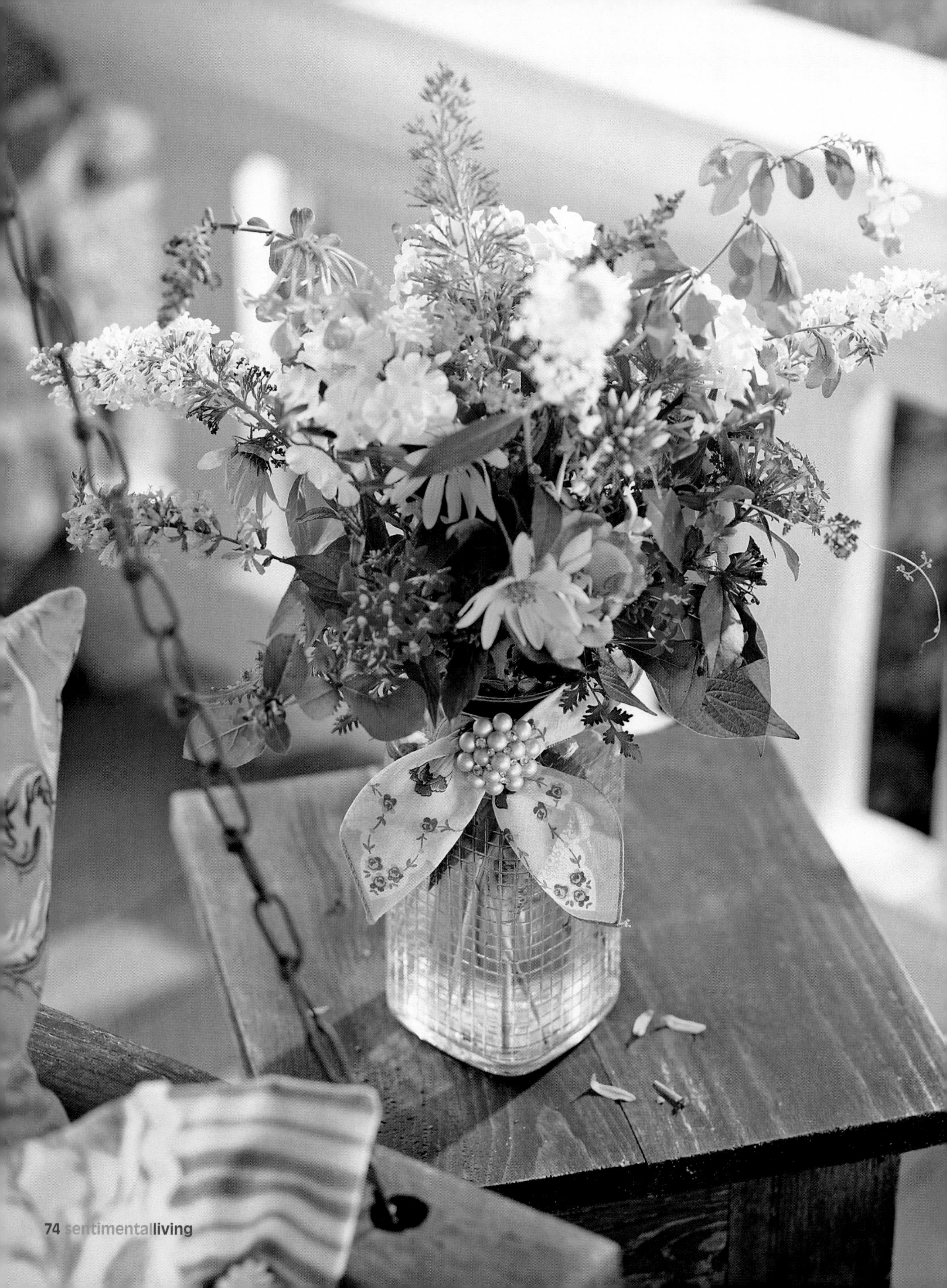

Mason jars are easily found in grandmother's attic, at tag sales, and antique markets. They are a staple to keep on hand, for they offer a variety of uses. Some favorites are those with windowpane embossing or a hint of blue in the glass. A Mason jar becomes a vase (opposite) when wrapped in an antique handkerchief that's clasped with a one-of-a-kind earring.

# *Turn the ordinary into the unique,*
## *and the run-of-the-mill into the charming.*

**Left:** Pretty seed packets and a hand spade with a painted handle are fertile topics for conversation. Glue a seed packet to the front of the jar, then tie raffia around the neck of the jar. Glue a raffia-threaded button to the tied raffia.

**Right:** To make a magical hanging lantern, form a ring of wire around the neck of a jar. Thread glass beads from an old necklace onto a second wire, then fasten the wire ends to the ring. Add sand and a scented candle.

**Bottom, right:** Scrapbook stickers instantly convert a jar into a firefly nightlight for a bedside table. Remember to punch tiny holes in the lid, and free the insects the next day.

*Below:* An armchair voyage is always at hand when you keep photos and other memorabilia in a Vacation Scrapbook.
*Right and opposite:* To hold larger travel mementos, use a Vacation Keepsake Valise.

On page 153, Alda shows you how to create both nostalgic memory keepers.

# VACATION
## *memories*

A sentimental journey doesn't have to end once the traveler reaches home. To keep the vacation memories close at hand, create a scrapbook filled with photographs, ticket stubs, and postcards. Or let a well-traveled suitcase hold guide books, pamphlets, roadmaps, and other souvenirs too large to display in an album. Looking through the memorabilia will renew the journey for an afternoon of armchair reminiscence on the porch.

Live life to the fullest.

Family Fun

Favorite places

The best of times

VACATION

KEEPSAKES

Discover

Wander

Play hard

# sentimental
## autumn
*a view from the porch*

When the air turns crisp, the porch offers an overflowing welcome, a place to sit with loved ones and view the display of colors. It is also the perfect spot for taking "First Day of School" photos with backpacks and lunch kits. On a chilly afternoon, linger in the porch swing and immerse yourself in a classic novel while warming your fingers on a mug of cider. Now is the time of year we all go home in our hearts.

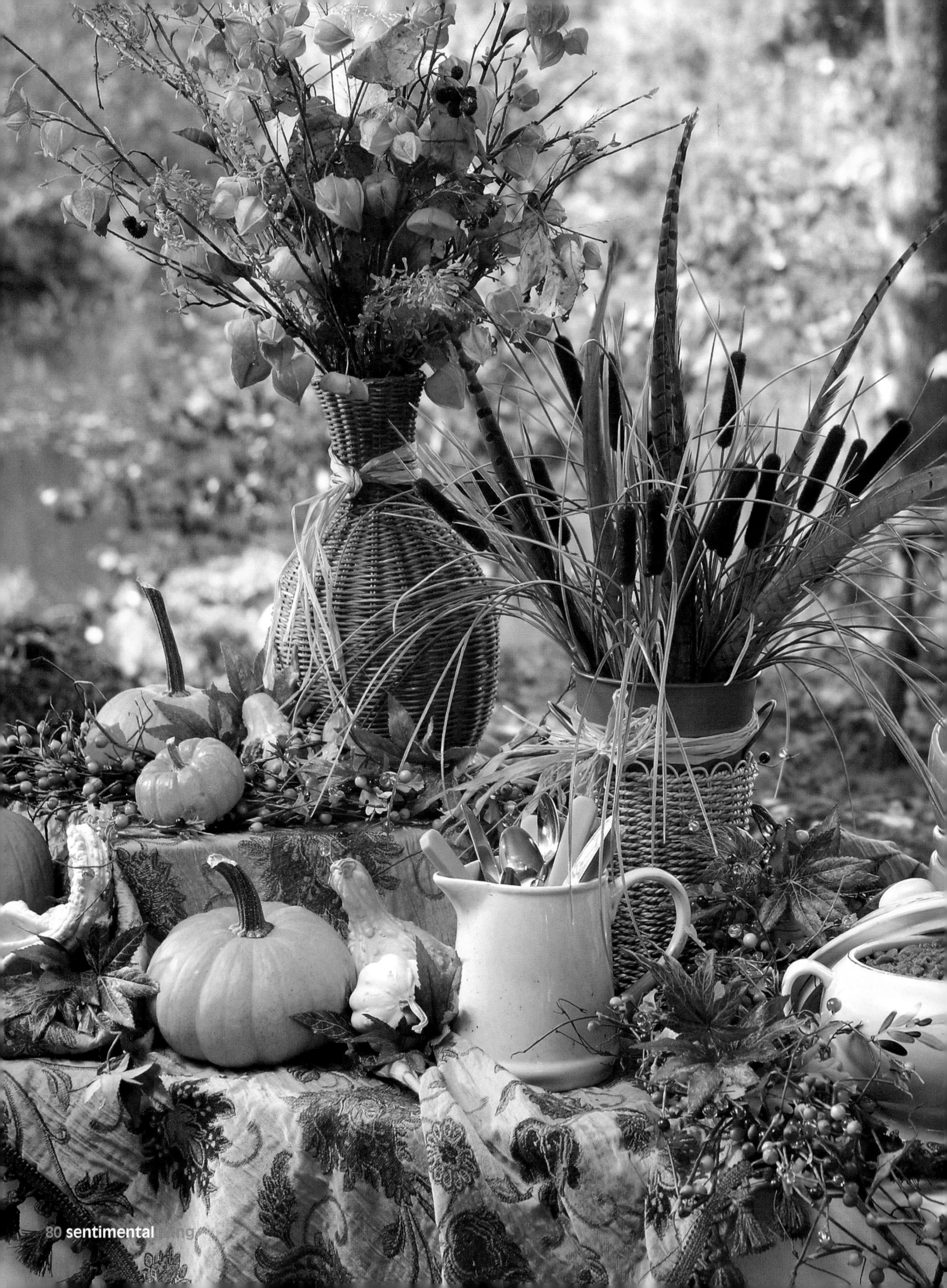

# Festivities

**The Menu**

**Hot Mulled Cider**

**Easy Chili**

**Best Ever Spinach Dip**

**Pecan Pie**

**Toasted Pumpkin Seeds**

Come, gather at our table ...
it has become a tradition for our family to
host an annual "Fall Fling," complete with
a bonfire, an abundance of good food, a
hayride, and a live band. Friends join us to
share in the fun. We enjoy quilts thrown
over willow chairs, the beauty of fall
colors, and an offering of hot chili and
warm cider. "Come, be our guest" is the
sentiment that autumn brings. And in the
season of thanksgiving, it is the true gift of
family and friends for which we rejoice.

Prepare an easy outdoor feast for your loved ones and
enjoy the blessings of time shared in the cool, autumn
air. See more of this fun and casual get-together on the
pages that follow. And turn to page 154 to make Alda's
No-Sew Table Throw.

"On a crisp October evening, gather to host a party for family and friends on the porch."

I grew up in the South, where a porch traditionally served as an extra room, especially when entertaining. To make the most of your evening, plan comforting foods that can be prepared ahead of time. It's better to enjoy the welcome warmth of conversation than to spend hours in the warmth of the kitchen. Present the meal in autumn style by scattering artificial berries and leaves over the table. And I think a hollowed-out pumpkin is the perfect bowl for my favorite spinach dip.

### Easy Chili
- 1 pound ground beef
- 1 tablespoon butter
- 1 medium onion, chopped
- 1 can (20 ounces) Mexican-style beans
- 1 can (10 ounces) cream of tomato soup
- 1 can (10 ounces) diced tomatoes and green chilies
- 1 teaspoon salt
- 1 tablespoon chili powder

Brown beef in skillet with butter and onion. Add remaining ingredients; simmer 1 hour.

Toppings:
shredded Cheddar cheese
chopped green onions
corn chips

### Best Ever Spinach Dip
- 1 package (10 ounces) chopped frozen spinach, thawed and drained
- 1 can (8 ounces) water chestnuts, drained and chopped coarsely
- 2 cups sour cream
- 3 tablespoons mayonnaise
- 1 package (1.4 ounces) dry vegetable soup mix
- 3 green onions, chopped

Mix all ingredients in a bowl and spoon into a medium-sized hollowed-out pumpkin. Serve with dip-sized corn chips.

*Place the pumpkin lid inside a rustic twig wreath next to the pumpkin. Add colorful fall leaves and you have the centerpiece too!*

### Hot Mulled Cider
- 1 gallon apple cider
- 1 cup orange juice
- $^1/_2$ cup red hots
- 4 3-inch cinnamon sticks, broken
- $^1/_2$ teaspoon ground nutmeg
- Garnish: orange slices

Prepare cider using a large automatic coffee maker. Substitute the cider for the water. Place remaining ingredients in the coffee basket and brew. Serve hot in tin enamel mugs, each topped with an orange slice.

**Opposite:** Alda serves her popular cool-weather drink, Hot Mulled Cider. Cheese, green onions, and corn chips are ready to top hearty servings of Easy Chili.
***This page:*** Savory dishes like Easy Chili and Best Ever Spinach Dip always disappear early in the evening.

# harvest
# TRADITIONS

The bounty we celebrate today is that of our loved ones, who, for a time, leave behind the often harried and frustrating world of business to share the joys of a hayride on a beautiful fall day. The gentle spirit of Sentimental Living enriches this harvest tradition … a family homecoming where we count our abundant blessings.

*Opposite:* Set up a festive dessert table laden with a variety of treats for the eyes, as well as the taste buds!
*This page:* Nothing whets appetites for fall foods better than a trip through the fields on an old-fashioned hayride.

toasted
pumpkin seeds

toasted
pumpkin seeds

## Pecan Pie

- 3 eggs, beaten
- ²/₃ cup sugar
- ¹/₃ teaspoon salt
- ¹/₃ cup butter, melted
- 1 cup maple-flavored pancake syrup
- 1 unbaked 9-inch pie shell
- 1 cup pecan halves

Combine eggs, sugar, salt, butter, and syrup in a medium-sized bowl and mix well. Pour mixture into pie shell and top with pecan halves. Bake at 375° for 45 minutes.

## Toasted Pumpkin Seeds

- 6 cups whole pumpkin seeds (not shelled)
- 3 tablespoons vegetable oil
- 1¹/₂ teaspoons salt
- ³/₄ teaspoon garlic salt

Rinse pumpkin seeds and pat dry with paper towel. Toss seeds with oil, then spread them out on cookie sheets. Tossing seeds every 5-7 minutes, bake at 360° for 20 minutes or until seeds are light golden brown. Remove from oven; pour into a clean paper bag. Pour salt in the bag. Holding the top tight, shake bag to salt seeds evenly. See page 154 to make Pumpkin Seed Favors.

Extra seating needn't be costly — use straw bales! After the party, spread the straw on your flower beds for mulch. This night ends on a sweet note with Pecan Pie and bluegrass music.

smell

# five SENSES of autumn

Stepping out onto the porch and smelling the first fire of the season makes me smile. When I see wood smoke curling from a campfire or a nearby chimney, to me it announces in a most elegant way that autumn is in the air. The crunch of leaves underfoot, the ringing of school bells, the sweetness of homemade pumpkin pie … the things we smell, touch, see, hear, and taste are those that we recall with a warm heart. Fall is a prelude to the holidays and to the busiest time of the year. Around Thanksgiving, we pause for a few moments to reconnect with family and friends. School children enjoy a break, college students have their first long weekend at home, and working adults get a day or two to relax. Together, we relish traditional foods. And later, we clasp autumn-chilled fingers around mugs of hot cider. The simple joys of the season are a reminder that a front porch gathering need not be lavish in design to be rich in memories.

*Opposite:* The mingled scents of toasted marshmallows and wood smoke create a fond childhood memory.
*This page:* Filled with hot cider, an enameled mug warms the fingers as well as the palate. Leaves glow in the colors of autumn. School bells call to the hearts of young and old alike. And who can resist the simple goodness of pumpkin pie?

touch  see  hear  taste

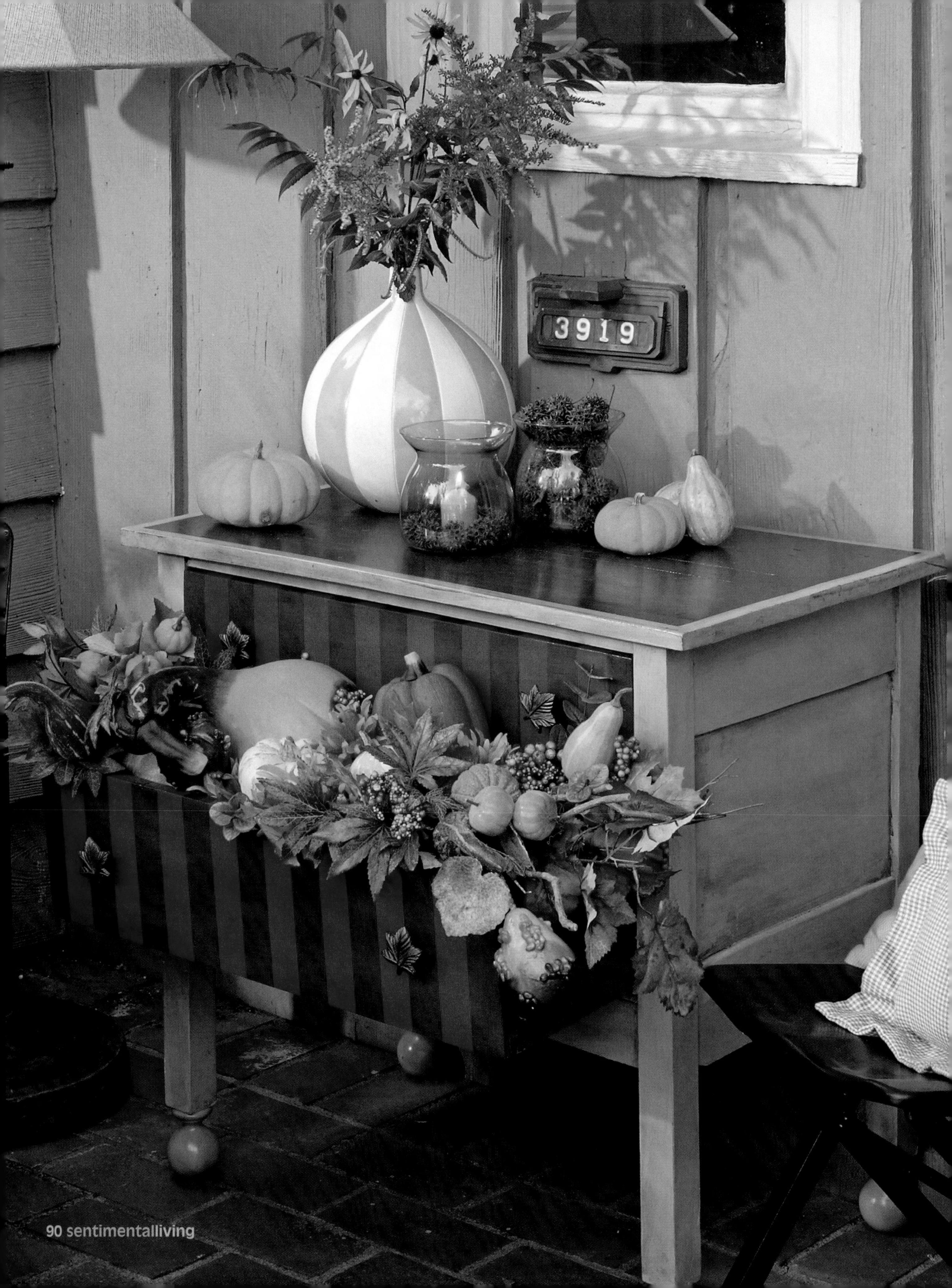
3919

**Opposite page:** A Painted Bureau offers extra space for autumn color. Alda shares the easy technique on page 155.
**This page:** The faux fruit on the Apple Wreath looks positively delicious. See page 154 to make your own refreshing décor.

Whether you're relaxing alone or entertaining friends, you'll find that a few personal touches make your outdoor room more inviting. Tablescapes are a great way to display collections. If a regular table is too large for your porch, use paint to awaken an old bureau, then let its bottom drawer catch the overflow of a brightly hued arrangement. Orange, red, green, and gold … these colors were inspired by a woodland stroll where I saw trees dressed in their richest foliage. Such abundance is also the theme of our apple wreath. It greets holiday guests with timeless style. When your porch is decorated for the season, hospitality beckons right outside your own front door.

# An Autumn
# WELCOME

**This page:** With her wooden wings, flower hair, and vintage pillowcase robe, the Autumn Angel assures guests that they are as welcome as the season. Alda makes the heavenly greeter on page 154.
**Opposite page:** Above the door, a floral swag is attached to a scrap of decorative ironwork from the flea market. The door baskets are also very simple to assemble — Alda lined each basket with black felt before adding a raffia bow and wire-edged ribbons for a hanger. She filled the baskets with floral foam, bittersweet, fall foliage, and sunflowers.

*A porch comes halfway to meet a guest, with outstretched hands, and bids him a lingering goodbye when he must go.*
— Dorothy Scarborough

# autumn
## FRIENDSHIP BASKET

Create an autumn ambience with seasonal gifts from the friendship basket. The individual cones are made from upholsterer's fabric and are rich with fall texture. I've filled them with sugared pecans, a treat that sends forth the sentiment "You're Special." Remember to keep your basket near the door, ready to share a gift that celebrates nature's bounty.

Tokens of friendship that will keep visitors coming back for more, Gift Cones are so very simple to create! Make them with Alda on page 155.

*Sugared Maple Pecans*
   2  egg whites
   6  tablespoons maple syrup
 1/4  teaspoon orange extract
   8  cups pecan halves
   1  cup firmly packed brown sugar
   1  teaspoon salt

Preheat oven to 225°. In a large bowl, beat egg whites until foamy. Beat in maple syrup and orange extract. Stir in pecan halves. Stir in brown sugar and salt. Spread pecans on lightly greased baking sheets. Bake 1 hour or until golden brown, stirring every 15 minutes. Cool on baking sheets. Store in an airtight container.

*A basket filled with treasures announces to your guests that cheery Autumn has arrived.*

— *Alda*

Flowers with red, orange, and gold petals make a beautiful fall bouquet. Mums are magnificent when snuggled inside pot covers made from old flannel shirts. To represent the season in a most memorable way, insert a water-filled jar into a hollowed-out pumpkin, then add roses in lovely autumnal colors.

*This page:* For fall displays, it's easy to locate a new basket at craft fairs. And check your rag bag for flannel shirts ... on page 156, Alda turns the worn garments into Fabric-Covered Pots. She also shares how to create Pinecone Fire Starters on page 155.
*Opposite page:* Ordinary jars come in many sizes, making it simple to convert any pumpkin into a charming autumn vase.

# *bountiful* bouquets

*This page:* Fill an Autumn Leaves Washtub with the bountiful colors of fall produce and flowers. But first, spread those same joyful hues on the outside of the tub. On page 156, Alda shows you how.
*Opposite:* Keep your cider sipping-hot with Mug Cozies on a Fabric-Lined Tray. And while you're enjoying the sights of autumn, listen to the gentle trickle of water cascading over a Pumpkin Fountain. Alda creates all three on page 156.

# What Autumn Brings

When the crisp autumn air settles on the dogwood tree, turning its leaves bright red, we see that Nature has created a painterly backdrop for all sorts of seasonal offerings. The best place to enjoy this gold and russet palette is on your own porch. Arrange little "still lifes" everywhere of fall produce and yellow mums. Or perhaps a pumpkin water fountain would "steal the show" while adding a soothing element of sound. Even on the porch, I like to mix silver accessories with earthenware mugs. A fabric lining warms the silver tray, and my favorite beverages stay hot longer when the mugs are wrapped in handmade cozies. These artful autumn touches are invitations to simply linger.

# *Going*

Autumn is a season for fun! Alda's lighthearted creations include a Punched Tin Lantern, Gourd Birdhouse, and Happy Halloween Table with Chairs. Instructions begin on page 156.

# *Round in*

Make the most of your porch with individual, whimsical touches that declare it your own. Gourds grown over the summer on a nearby fence become wonderful little birdhouses. A coffee can makes a quick transition into a hanging lantern … a nice enhancement to autumnal evenings on the porch. Fashion several of the instant candleholders so you'll have extras to give as gifts. For a hauntingly pleasant visit, welcome guests with a hand-painted table and folding chairs with dish-towel cushions.

Circles

2210

# cute & cozy...

## fall creations

Enrich your outdoor living with emblems of the season — brightly colored leaves, candy corn, and scarecrows. A fall afghan that beautifully displays autumn leaves is a bit of luxury when tossed over the corner of a chair. Pillows of fleecy candy corn — so simple to create — brighten up a weathered bench. A scarecrow pillow is also easy to make, yet full of personality as he welcomes us with his rickrack smile.

**Opposite page:** Mr. Scarecrow Pillow will inspire lots of giggles and grins. And who wouldn't "fall" for the cute Candy Corn Pillows? Alda makes them all in a jiffy on page 157.
**This page:** Crochet Alda's Autumn Afghan one square at a time. It's a perfect project for a creative day spent on-the-go — or on the porch! Instructions begin on page 158.

The unexpected sight of nature's treasures gathered for display will make guests smile as they walk onto your porch. On a woodland stroll, you can acquire lichen-trimmed branches, mounds of moss, or bright green hedge apples from a bois d'arc tree. Another favorite arrangement for fall is that of colorful leaf branches and berries on twigs. Or make a trip to the farmer's market to get pumpkins, gourds, and Indian corn. Any of these natural beauties will announce to visitors that fall has happily arrived.

*gatherings*

*Opposite:* With the days growing shorter, candles are ever more important. Apples or miniature pumpkins make charming votive or tea light candle holders for a party. Use a sharp knife to cut a hole slightly larger than the candle's base in the top of the apple or pumpkin. Display your "natural" candles atop a mound of hedge apples. And of course, never leave burning candles unsupervised.
*Above:* For instant fall color, set out a rustic bowlful of gourds and Indian corn. See page 159 to create your own Crackled Bowl.
*Left:* Roadside beauties seem to burst from the top of this old watering can. On its own, each stem or branch is a common element of nature — but just look what you have when they're placed together!

# SCARING up a little FUN

A homemade scarecrow serves as our official greeter to all those who pass by. Fred, as we lovingly call him, is dressed in thrift store finery. He weathers quite nicely. I save the scarecrow body from year to year, adding a little more fluff as it settles. If he gets wet, he just dries in the sun. I leave space beside Fred so children can sit or stand next to him, which creates an ideal setting for a "Kodak Picture Moment." Against a backdrop of cornstalks, hay bales, and mums, Mr. Scarecrow enjoys the company of a dressed-up pumpkin turkey and some spooky tin can spiders. It's a memory for the making.

**Opposite:** A Pumpkin Turkey is a humorous transition between Halloween and Thanksgiving. And although you'll never find real spiderwebs on her porch, Alda is quite fond of her Spider Candle Holders! To make the fun decorations, see page 159. **This page:** Let Fred Scarecrow greet your guests. On page 160, you can see how Alda assembled Fred.

# Classic Comforts

The front porch need not be lavish to be rich in memories. Enjoy a day immersed in the companionship of books, for reading becomes a respite from a hurried life. A quilt as warm as a mother's hug is the perfect accompaniment to a front porch afternoon. Keep a letter opener for opening the day's mail and a magnifying glass for inspecting small treasures from a nature walk.

**This page:** If you love to read in the fresh air, you may wish to make brown paper dust jackets for your favorite novels. Other handy things to keep nearby while perusing the pages: apples for munching, a letter opener and magnifying glass for important communiqués, and a warm beverage to enjoy with fresh-baked mini muffins.
**Opposite:** A quilt and a rocking chair — two front porch classics that are especially welcome in the fall.

Quilts courtesy of Nan Slaughter.

Warm pumpkin bread and herbal tea are wonderful refreshments for an autumn afternoon on the porch. The sentimental recipe is a delicious way to keep memories of home in your heart.

# A Slice of the Season

**This page:** Baked in a coffee can, Pumpkin Bread is beautiful when sliced — and especially so when slathered in cream cheese! **Opposite page:** To give as a gift, simply wrap the bread in cellophane and tie it with pretty ribbons, then add a color photocopy of our label on page 161.

*Pumpkin Bread*

$3^1/2$ cups sifted all-purpose flour
2 teaspoons soda
$1^1/2$ teaspoons salt
2 teaspoons cinnamon
2 teaspoons nutmeg
3 cups sugar
4 eggs, beaten
$^2/_3$ cup water
1 cup salad oil
2 cups (16-ounce can) pumpkin
1 cup pecans, chopped

Combine flour, soda, salt, cinnamon, nutmeg, and sugar in a large mixing bowl. Add eggs, water, oil, and pumpkin. Stir until blended. Add nuts and mix well. Butter and flour three 1-pound coffee cans. Pour mixture evenly into cans. Bake 1 hour at 350°. Cool slightly in cans and turn out on cooling rack to cool completely.

FAMILY

*memories*

Fall Festival
at the
Ellis Home

HAPPY
FALL

HEY! A HAYRIDE!

**Opposite:** See pages 160 and 161 to save the highlights of the season on Scrapbook Pages. **This page:** Alda used cardstock and a photocopy of the design on page 174 to create the mat for the Postcard Frame (page 161).

**S**eason's bounty … the blessings of friendship and the love of family are treasures we should preserve. Our autumn harvest home plays host every year to an annual "Fall Fling," complete with bonfire and hayride. As you can see, an old-fashioned event such as this presents many special moments to the camera. Protect a favorite photo in a custom-matted frame, or begin a scrapbook to keep your snapshots forever pressed within the pages of time.

# sentimental winter

*a view from the porch*

Winter not only brings Christmas and all its attendant glory, it also provides plentiful reasons to have fun. I look forward to the celebrations of winter events on the porch, whether I'm hosting carolers, a sledding party, or a New Year's Eve fireworks display. And of course there are the joyous reunions — nothing is more dear than the hugs of loved ones who've been away too long! In winter, I like to linger on my porch to watch the snow fall … it's always a promise of magical days to come.

# *perfect* Harmony

Just because the weather is cold, it doesn't mean that friendships can't be warmer than ever! Heat up the neighborhood by hosting a winter Caroling Party for children. You provide the fun decorations and the kid-friendly snacks — the youngsters provide the entertainment. It's a wonderful way to welcome the holidays, make new friends, and celebrate a season that's meant to be shared and enjoyed.

Even if snow is a rarity in your region, you can still have plenty of frosty fun! Whimsical decorations such as the snowflake garland and frosty wreaths will help you start the Yuletide season. If you leave the colorful décor in place all winter, you'll encourage smiles to linger as long as the air is chilly.

**The Menu**

Peanut Butter Snowballs

Sugar Cookies

Triple Chocolate Cocoa Mix

Remarkable Fudge

Share the preparations for your Caroling Party and double the fun by co-hosting with a neighbor, friend, or relative. If you serve a variety of treats that may be picked up by the handful, the carolers will feel well rewarded for their gifts of music. Serve popcorn tossed with colorful sour candies and fill a bucket with cookies. The memories you'll make on a cold winter porch will warm your heart for a lifetime.

*This page:* Alda and her sister, Cheryl, dish up a popcorn and sour-candy snack mix for the young choristers.
*Opposite, top:* Mr. and Mrs. Snowman, with their frosted-twig hair and cheery smiles, take center stage on the serving table. Along with the Fleece Table Runner and Snow-Lined Mugs, these decorations are completely no-sew. Alda makes them all on page 162.
*Opposite, bottom:* Peanut Butter Snowballs are super-fast cookies to make, and they're likely to disappear just as quickly!

## *Peanut Butter Snowballs*

 1 cup creamy peanut butter
 1 package (11 ounces) vanilla wafers
 16 ounces vanilla candy coating
   white coarse decorating sugar

Spread about 1 teaspoon peanut butter on flat side of 1 cookie; top with second cookie. Repeat using remaining cookies and peanut butter. Melt candy coating in the top of a double boiler over simmering water. Remove from heat. (If candy coating begins to harden, return to heat.) Place each cookie sandwich on a fork and hold over pan; spoon candy coating over cookie. Transfer to waxed paper. Sprinkle cookies with sugar before coating hardens. Allow coating to harden. Store in an airtight container in a cool place.

### Sugar Cookies

1¹/₄ cups all-purpose flour (sifted before you measure)
¹/₄ teaspoon baking powder
¹/₄ teaspoon salt
¹/₂ cup shortening
³/₄ cup sugar
1 egg
1 tablespoon milk
1 teaspoon vanilla
star, snowman, and mitten cookie cutters
colored sugar

Sift together flour, baking powder, and salt. Cream shortening, add sugar gradually, and cream until light and fluffy. Add egg and beat. Mix in milk and vanilla. Stir in dry ingredients. Chill dough. Roll to ¹/₈-inch thickness and cut with cookie cutters. Place on a baking sheet lined with parchment paper and sprinkle with sugar. Bake at 400° for 5 to 7 minutes.

*Left:* They're so simple to create, you may decide to give a Fleece Scarf and a Snow-Lined Mug to all the children you know! Instructions for these winter warmers are on page 162. Alda includes the how-tos and artwork for the Songbook on pages 162 and 175.
*Below:* Alda's old-fashioned Sugar Cookies fill a festive jar. The "label" is simply an enlarged photocopy of the Songbook design, trimmed and glued in place.

The children appreciate the warmth of easy-to-make fleece scarves as they stroll from house to house sharing their glad tidings. To ensure that each chorister knows the words to every tune, create colorful songbooks. These double as keepsakes of a fun-filled day. Even Lady, the dog, knows there is something special in the air.

## Triple Chocolate Cocoa Mix

- 6 cups nonfat milk powder
- 1 package (16 ounces) confectioner's sugar
- 2 jars (8 ounces each) Swiss chocolate-flavored non-dairy powdered creamer
- 1 package (15 ounces) chocolate mix for milk
- $^1/_4$ cup unsweetened cocoa powder
- 1 teaspoon salt

Combine all ingredients in a very large bowl. To serve, pour 6 ounces hot water over 3 tablespoons cocoa mix; stir until well blended. Store leftover mix in an airtight container in refrigerator.

For a minty twist, add one $7^1/_2$-ounce package of round peppermint candies, finely ground, to your cocoa mix.

# "The chill of winter, the warmth of friends...."

## Remarkable Fudge

- 4 cups sugar
- 1 can (12 ounces) evaporated milk
- 1 stick butter
- 1 package (12 ounces) semi-sweet chocolate chips
- 1 teaspoon vanilla
- 1 jar (7 ounces) marshmallow cream
- 1 cup walnuts (or pecans), chopped

Combine sugar, milk, and butter in a heavy pan. Cook over medium heat, stirring to prevent sticking. When butter is melted and all ingredients are well mixed, bring mixture to a boil. Boil for 5 minutes, stirring constantly. Remove from heat; add chocolate chips, vanilla, marshmallow cream, and nuts. Beat until chips are melted and blended. Pour into a buttered 13" x 9" x 2" pan. Refrigerate overnight and cut into squares.

Triple Chocolate Cocoa Mix and Remarkable Fudge are two yummy treats that will satisfy any sweet tooth.

smell

hear          see          touch          taste

# five SENSES of winter

In winter, our senses are heightened by the excitement of the holidays. Although we may not remember the gifts we received at Christmas last year, we do remember gathering fragrant greenery after the first snowfall. We clearly recall the smell of sugar cookies that were baked with the help of a visiting grandmother. We celebrate the joy of the season by listening for the bells of winter. Jingle bells, doorbells, sleigh bells, and church bells — they provide a chorus of good cheer to accompany the traditions that bring family and friends together. It is also pleasant to engage in a moment of solitude on the front porch and see the candles glow and the Christmas lights twinkle. Even the tastes of winter seem better outside … an enamel dishpan full of buttery popcorn to munch while you watch the children sledding. Or bring a toasty cup of cocoa and a plate of cookies onto the porch. And don't forget to make some snow ice cream!

*Opposite:* A basket filled with fresh greenery from the woods is a memory in the making.
*This page:* Jingle bells announce each visitor with their merry ring. A window brightened with candle glow is a welcoming sight. And although fingers get chilled, hearts always thrill to the fun of shaping snow into friendly missiles. What's the best way to end a winter day? Homemade sugar cookies!

Holiday
Howdy!

RAINBO IS BREAD

# A WINTER
## *welcome*

Simple yet heartfelt greetings brighten the winter holidays for everyone. Whether you welcome front door guests or back door friends and family, an entryway decoration that shares the sentiment "Love and Joy Come to You" will also speak volumes about your hospitality. Make the most of every opportunity to shower the Christmas spirit on all those you know. This year, even our bunkhouse looks festive with evergreen garland and a horse collar wreath. This is so visitors who wander out to see our horses will also find a bit of seasonal cheer. For Yuletide decorating, make the most of whatever you have on hand or whatever you find at a flea market. You'll be guaranteed a sentimental Christmas.

*Opposite:* When you love Christmas, it shows! A hearty "howdy" on a Horse Collar Wreath leaves no doubt that guests are welcome to enjoy this country display. The collar was a treasure from the flea market. Instructions for the sign are on page 164.
*Above:* A flea market find of a different kind — an inverted tray, freshly painted in white and stenciled with gold letters, declares a happy wish beside the front door. How-tos are on page 164.

*This page:* Old mittens, gloves, and ice skates make playful decorations.
*Opposite:* Holiday décor may be growing in your yard! Clip branches from an evergreen shrub, then follow Alda's instructions on page 164 to shape your monogram.

# With Memories Attached

Perhaps the best decorations are those that have memories attached.
Outgrown mittens adorn a garland over the back door. The ice skates are
from my friend Patti, who as a schoolgirl practiced perfect "eights" on a frozen
pond up North. Even the sleds have been passed down from one generation
to another. On our front door, the wreath is actually an evergreen monogram.
The branches were clipped from a hundred-year-old boxwood on the lawn.

# *winter*
## FRIENDSHIP BASKET

A friendship basket by the entryway brightens up the dark winter months, for even with all the flurry of guests coming and going, attentive touches will not go unnoticed. Have the season's warmest wishes at heart and share the message of hospitality and welcome to all those who enter your front door.

Guests will feel truly blessed to receive these Gift Boxes filled with a bounty of Clouds. The foil candy boxes were found in the cake decorating department of an arts and crafts store. Photocopy the angel on page 175 to make your own gift tags.

*Clouds*
  1  18.5-ounce white cake mix
  1  egg, beaten
  1  8-ounce container frozen
     whipped topping,
     thawed
  3  cups powdered sugar

Combine cake mix and egg. Fold in whipped topping. Drop by teaspoonfuls into powdered sugar and coat well. Place on ungreased cookie sheet. Bake at 350° for 8-10 minutes or until tops are firm.

*Hospitality is a gift of your time. The most treasured gift you can make for your family and friends is a memory.*
— Alda

# MAKE
# WINTER
# GLOW

*Opposite:* Put your candles on a pedestal — this elevated candelabra is actually a chandelier placed atop a stand for a garden gazing ball. Faux moss and berry candle-rings add color to the outdoor decoration. Use a glue appropriate for the materials when securing the chandelier to the stand.

*Above:* When you use candle oil and your favorite items from nature, you can create an expensive-looking Jar Lantern. On page 164, Alda uses key limes to create this radiant example.

*Right:* Candlelight symbolically removes winter's chill, especially when the radiance spills from an old ice bucket. Cranberries add seasonal cheer and keep the candle centered.

Evening falls early in winter months, so what better reason to fill your porch with candlelight? Whether casual or formal, a candlescape greets visitors in the dark of winter with a warm, shining glow. I've adopted the tradition of candlelight in my Southern home, for it is a signal of hospitality.

*This page:* Enjoy fresh air even when it's chilly outside. The Faux Fur Throw is backed in wool fabric for a wrap that's extra-warm. Alda's quick instructions are on page 164. *Opposite:* To help you lounge in comfort, turn to page 163 to knit a pair of winter-white pillows. You'll welcome their classic appearance year-round.

# COOL-WEATHER

Even in the depths of winter, I find myself called outdoors to enjoy warm creature comforts on the patio. A change of fabrics is all it takes to make the seasonal transition. I cover chairs with faux fur blankets lined in plaid wool. Holly-berry red is a color that can take you through the Yuletide season and still brighten up wintry afternoons long afterwards. A perfect pastime for such days is knitting. These cozy knit pillows remind me of my sons' old Christmas sweaters, making them a sentimental favorite.

# COMFORTS

*candles*

With just a quick change of color and ribbon, Alda's
Hurricane Lanterns adapt to any decorating theme. See page
165 to learn how easily you can make your home shine.

# to light the way

There is perhaps no decorative element more magical, elegant, or gracious than
candlelight. Here, hurricane lanterns line a walkway to welcome guests. To set a
gala mood as night falls, a pair of lanterns in an antique urn will bathe the front
door in candle glow. The base for each of Alda's handmade lanterns is
surprisingly created using the most humble of materials … a tuna can and a
wooden dowel! These simple-to-make lights are embellished with ribbons,
turning an ordinary sidewalk into a grand entryway. You will want to make several!

# For the birds

### After our family has enjoyed a real Christmas tree indoors,

we "plant" it outside and redecorate its branches with winter treats for the birds. Position your tree where you can watch through your window and see the birds and squirrels dine on the abundance of your offerings. On winter's coldest of days, these treats bring a feast of plenty to God's smallest creatures.

## Bird Seed Wreath
- 1 cup bacon drippings
- 2 cups birdseed

Grease 4-inch ring molds and 3½-inch heart molds with vegetable spray. Melt bacon drippings in the microwave. Stir in birdseed and fill molds. Push the mixture in with the tips of your fingers to fill mold completely and eliminate air bubbles. While mixture is still wet, place a small wooden dowel at center of mold and use a stirring motion to make a 1-inch diameter hole in mixture. Place in refrigerator for two hours to chill. Run a sharp knife around the inside edge of the molds to release wreaths. Use paper twine to hang wreaths outside for the birds, or store them in plastic wrap in the refrigerator if you plan to give them as gifts.

## Winter Treat for the Birds
- 2 cups bacon drippings or suet
- 1 cup sunflower seeds
- 1 cup wild bird seed mix
  hollowed-out orange halves

Melt bacon drippings or suet in a sauce pan; stir in all seeds. Threading cranberries on twine if desired, add a jute or paper twine hanger to each orange half. Spoon mixture into orange halves placed on a muffin tin to keep upright. Cool in the refrigerator until solid. Use any leftover mixture to "ice" pinecones. Knot twine around the pinecones for hangers.

*Opposite page:* For a garland the birds will enjoy, string cranberries and popcorn on paper twine.

PAWS-ITIVELY

Say the word "puppy" to me and I lose all reason! Maggie, my little rescue dog in the lavender sweater, ceased to be an animal long ago. Instead, she is a cherished member of our family. I think it's only natural to lavish affection on a beloved pet, perhaps in the form of a hand-knitted sweater like Maggie's, or maybe as a jeweled velvet collar or a pillow bed. It has been said that dogs are not our whole lives, but they certainly help to make our lives whole.

# sentimental

*Opposite:* Glue a length of beaded fringe onto the back of a velvet ribbon. Your best furry friend will have a stylish new collar.
*Above:* Want to earn lots of extra puppy kisses? Knit a Dog Sweater for your four-legged pal. You'll find Alda's pattern in several sizes on page 165.
*Left:* Dogs of all ages will have tail-wagging dreams on a bed that's covered with a Doggie Duvet. On page 165, fleece fabric warms up your pet's pillow bed for the ultimate in canine comfort.

With their hearts still glowing from memories of Christmas, January visitors love to see these happy snowman greeters. No sewing skills are needed to make the friendly creations. I just cut pieces of felt and fleece, glued and fused them together, then added button smiles. And now, whatever the forecast may bring, my porch will be cheery and bright.

# porch BRIGHTENERS in "SNOW" time

*Opposite:* When nature settles in for a long winter's nap, it doesn't mean your porch must become drab and dreary. Turn to page 166 to see how you can bring your front door to life with a colorful Snowman Banner.
*Left:* Just for fun, toss this Friendly Snow Fellow over the back of a chair. On page 167, Alda puts this fleece outdoor décor together in record time, and you can, too!
*Above:* No snow? No problem! See page 166 to make Faux Snowballs that will still be just as fluffy when the mercury rises. Instructions for the Snowman Bucket are on page 166.

# shining

# memories

Use meaningful images from the past to share a sentimental welcome. For example, the pineapple has been a symbol of hospitality since colonial times. In those days, ship's captains placed pineapples on their

gateposts. The exotic fruit was a signal of their return from the sea, and it invited neighbors to drop in for a visit. These paper luminaries will also make your guests feel welcomed and appreciated.

**Opposite, top:** See page 167 to make holiday candles glow in just minutes using vintage greeting cards.
**Opposite, bottom:** To create luminaries that shine with hospitality, purchase wallpaper cutouts in a pineapple print, then follow the instructions on page 167 to create Brown Bag Luminaries.
**This page:** When Alda's sister gifted her with photos from their childhood, Alda decided to create a Memory Tree. See page 167 for how-tos.

## *tip*

To display Gift Jars in your Friendship Basket, line bottom of basket with ice-filled zip-top plastic bags. Cover bags with fabric or a towel, then place jars in basket.

## 1 Door Pocket
*(shown on page 26)*

You will need acrylic paint, paintbrushes, metal wall pocket, sandpaper, spray adhesive, photocopy of a card, matte clear acrylic sealer, paper doily, silk flower bush, and ribbon.

*Use adhesive in a well-ventilated area.* Paint pocket; allow to dry. For an aged look, use sandpaper to remove paint in spots. Use spray adhesive to glue photocopy to pocket. Apply sealer; allow to dry. Arrange doily and flowers in pocket. Tie pocket handle to doorknob with ribbon.

## 2 Chalkboard Tray
*(shown on page 29)*

You will need painter's masking tape, a metal tray with filigree border (ours measures $18^1/_2$"w x $13^1/_2$"h x $1^3/_4$"d), black chalkboard paint, paintbrush, $1^1/_2$"w purple and gold variegated wire-edged ribbon, hot glue gun, and a silk hydrangea cluster and leaves removed from stem.

*Use caution when working with glue gun.*
1. Mask off inner sides of tray. Paint bottom of tray with chalkboard paint; allow to dry, then remove tape.
2. For hanger, knot ends of a length of ribbon around filigree border. Notch ribbon ends.
3. Hot glue hydrangea cluster and leaves to top edge of tray.

## 3 Gift Jars
*(shown on page 30)*

You will need ten $1/_2$-pint jelly jars filled with Raspberry Honey (recipe on page 30), white cardstock, $1/_8$" dia. hole punch, decorative paper, and twine.

For each jar, photocopy design, page 170, onto cardstock; cut into a $1^1/_2$" x $2^3/_4$" tag. Punch a hole in corner of tag. Cut a 5" square from decorative paper. Wrap paper over top of jar. Knot a length of twine around paper. Thread tag onto twine, then tie twine into a bow.

## 4 Spring Afghan
*(shown on page 32)*

Finished Size: $48^1/_2$" x 60" (123 cm x 152.5 cm)

*Read Knit and Crochet Basics, pages 168 – 169, before beginning Afghan.*

### MATERIALS

Worsted Weight Yarn:
[$3^1/_2$ ounces, 166 yards (100 grams, 152 meters) per ball]: 14 balls
31" (78.5 cm) circular knitting needle, size 11 (8 mm) **or** size needed for gauge

**GAUGE:** In pattern, 12 sts and 16 rows = 4" (10 cm)

Afghan is worked from top to bottom using two strands of yarn.
When instructed to slip a stitch, always slip as if to **purl**.

### AFGHAN
With two strands of yarn, cast on 146 sts.

**Row 1**: P1, [YO (**Fig. 2, page 169**), P2 tog (**Fig 3, page 169**)] across to last st, P1.
**Row 2** (Right side): K2, ★ YO, K2, [slip 1, K1, PSSO (**Fig. 4, page 169**)], K2 tog (**Fig. 5, page 169**), K2, YO, K1; repeat from ★ across.
**Row 3**: Purl across.
**Row 4**: K1, YO, K2, slip 1, K1, PSSO, K2 tog, K2, ★ YO, K1, YO, K2, slip 1, K1, PSSO, K2 tog, K2; repeat from ★ across to last 2 sts, YO, K2.
**Row 5**: Purl across.
Repeat Rows 2-5 until Afghan measures approximately 59" (150 cm) from cast on edge, ending by working Row 5.
**Next Row**: Slip 1, K1, PSSO, YO, K2, slip 1, K1, PSSO, ★ K2 tog, K2, YO, K1, YO, K2, slip 1, K1, PSSO; repeat from ★ across to last 5 sts, K2 tog, K1, YO, K2 tog: 144 sts.
**Next Row**: Purl across.
**Next Row**: [Slip 1, K2 tog, PSSO (**Fig. 6, page 169**), YO] twice, ★ (K2 tog, YO) 3 times, slip 1, K2 tog, PSSO, YO; repeat from ★ across to last 3 sts, K3 tog (**Fig. 7, page 169**): 125 sts.
**Last Row**: P2 tog, YO, P1, (YO, P2 tog) across.
Bind off all sts in **knit**.

**Design by Rena V. Stevens**

## 5 Pillows
*(shown on page 33)*

You will need a 14" dia. round and a 14" square no-sew decorator pillow form, 1½ yds each of pink and purple decorator fabric, hot glue gun, and two oversized silk flowers removed from stems.

*Use caution when working with glue gun.* Follow pillow form manufacturer's instructions to cut fabric and cover pillow forms. Hot glue a flower to center of each pillow.

## 6 Teacup Wreath
*(shown on page 35)*

You will need an artificial greenery wreath and assorted ribbons, teacups, and silk flowers.

Hang wreath, then use ribbons to tie teacups to wreath through handles. Insert stems of flowers through wreath. Tie ribbons into bows on wreath.

## 7 Chair Covers
*(shown on page 36)*

For each chair, you will need paper-backed fusible web, fabric for monogram, a fabric chair cover, fabric glue, pom-pom fringe, and ribbon.

Print desired letter from computer at desired size; cut out letter. Turn letter over and draw around it on paper side of fusible web. Fuse letter to wrong side of fabric; cut out. Remove paper backing and fuse fabric letter to chair cover. Glue fringe along bottom edge of chair cover. Tie bows with ribbon; glue bows to chair cover.

## 8 Urn
*(shown on page 37)*

You will need dark, medium, and light gray acrylic paints; a foam plate; natural sponge piece; plastic urn; matte clear acrylic sealer; and a paintbrush.

Pour all three paint shades, side by side, onto foam plate. Dampen sponge; dip sponge in paint, mixing the colors as you pick up the paint. Blot sponge on a paper towel to remove excess paint, then lightly dab sponge on urn, turning sponge so all three colors are applied randomly. Repeat until you achieve desired coverage; allow to dry. Apply sealer and allow to dry.

## 9 Bell Jars
*(shown on page 37)*

For each jar, you will need a large glass hurricane vase (found in candle section at craft stores), 24-gauge silver wire, wire cutters, pliers, ⅝" dia. bead, and a 1¼"h x 1¼" dia. clear glass knob.

1. With vase upside down, wrap two lengths of wire around tapered area of vase; tightly twist wire ends together. Trim excess wire.
2. For handle, thread bead onto center of two wire lengths. Twist 1" of wire together below bead. Thread wire ends through knob. Place knob and bead at center of vase bottom. Thread wire ends under wire at opposite sides of vase; tightly twist wire around itself to secure. Trim excess wire.

## 10 Catalog Basket
*(shown on page 38)*

You will need ⅛ yd striped fabric, ⅞"w fusible web tape, 8¼" x 12¾" piece of denim with pocket (ours is from a pair of overalls), liquid fray preventative, hot glue gun, and a woven basket (ours measures 16⅞"w x 9¾"h).

*Yardage is based on fabric with a 40" usable width. Use caution when working with glue gun.*

1. From striped fabric, cut two 3½" x 12¾" strips for side borders and one 3⅝" x 9" strip for bottom border. Fuse web tape along one long edge on wrong side of each strip. Matching wrong sides and overlapping edges of denim by 1", fuse side borders to denim, then center and fuse bottom border to denim.

2. Press each side border 1" to wrong side. Fuse web tape along right side of fold. Overlapping edges of denim, press and fuse side borders 1" to wrong side again. Repeat pressing and fusing instructions for bottom border. Apply fray preventative to raw fabric edges at bottom of pocket.
3. Fuse web tape along top edge on wrong side of pocket; fuse top edge 1" to wrong side. Gluing excess to bottom of basket, hot glue pocket to basket front.

## 11 Fish Fountain
*(shown on page 39)*

You will need polished stones and other small stones, a 19" dia. flowerpot saucer, tabletop fountain pump kit, ½" dia. plastic tubing, and a hollow glazed-ceramic fish with open mouth and hole in bottom to fit over pump. (If the hole in the bottom of your fish is not large enough to fit over pump, gently tap around the hole with a tack hammer, chipping away small pieces until the fish fits over the pump.)

Arrange stones in saucer. Place pump in saucer; attach tubing. Running tubing through hole in bottom of fish and out of mouth, place fish in bowl over pump. Trim tubing to fit to edge of mouth. Follow pump manufacturer's instructions to add water and operate pump.

*tip*

For a more durable outside surface for your suitcase or tray table, consider having a piece of glass custom cut to size.

## 12 Ottoman
*(shown on page 42)*

You will need a square storage ottoman, acrylic paint, paintbrush, two coordinating fabrics, $^7/_8$"w fusible web tape, hot glue gun, staple gun, and gimp trim.

*Use caution when working with glue gun.*
1. Remove feet from ottoman; paint feet as desired and allow to dry.
2. Measure around base of ottoman; add 2". Measure height of ottoman; add 3". Cut a piece of fabric the determined measurements.
3. For hem, fuse web tape on wrong side of fabric piece along one short edge. Fuse edge 1" to wrong side.
4. Overlapping and gluing short edges together with hemmed edge on top, center and wrap fabric around ottoman. Wrap and glue excess fabric at top to inside of ottoman. Pulling fabric taut, wrap and staple excess fabric to bottom of ottoman. Trim excess fabric. Reattach feet.
5. Glue gimp trim over raw fabric edges inside ottoman.
6. To cover lid piece, measure from bottom of lid, up one side, across top, and down remaining side; add 2". Cut a square of fabric this size.
7. Place top of lid on wrong side of fabric. Folding at corners, pull fabric taut to inside of lid and staple in place along inside edge.

## 13 Suitcase End Table
*(shown on page 42)*

You will need sandpaper, a wooden bench (ours measures $20^1/_4$"w x $17^1/_4$"h x $10^1/_2$"d), spray primer, vintage suitcase to fit on bench, white spray paint, matte clear acrylic spray sealer, fabric, spray adhesive, craft glue, and $^3/_8$"w white gimp trim.

*Use spray primer, paint, sealer, and adhesive in a well-ventilated area. Allow primer, paint, and sealer to dry after each application.*
Sand bench; prime bench and suitcase. Paint bench and suitcase white; apply sealer. Cut a piece of fabric to fit top side of suitcase. Use spray adhesive to glue fabric to suitcase. Use craft glue to glue trim over raw fabric edges. Arrange suitcase on bench.

## 14 Tray Side Table
*(shown on page 43)*

You will need sandpaper, a round metal tray with wooden folding stand (our tray measures $19^1/_4$" dia. and our stand measures $18^1/_2$"w x $17^3/_4$"h), spray primer, white and pink spray paints, matte clear acrylic spray sealer, polka-dot fabric, spray adhesive, craft glue, $^3/_8$"w white gimp trim, and pink jumbo rickrack.

*Use spray primer, paint, sealer, and adhesive in a well-ventilated area. Allow primer, paint, and sealer to dry after each application.*
Sand tray and stand; apply primer. Paint tray white and stand pink; apply sealer. Cut a circle from fabric to fit in bottom of tray. Use spray adhesive to glue fabric to tray. Use craft glue to glue gimp trim over raw edge of fabric circle; glue rickrack along edge of tray. Place tray on stand.

## 15 Album
*(shown on page 46)*

To make an heirloom keepsake, cut the decorative border from an embroidered pillowcase to accent an album. Center the decorative border on the front of the album, then fold and glue the raw edges to the inside; glue lengths of trim or ribbon over the raw edges. We laced a coordinating ribbon through the eyelet closure of our envelope-style album.

## 16 Stationery
*(shown on pages 46 – 47)*

You will need embroidered linens (such as doilies and handkerchiefs), decorative-edged craft scissors, assorted scrapbook papers, purchased blank cards and envelopes, and spray adhesive.

*Use adhesive in a well-ventilated area.*
Make color photocopies of linens. Use craft scissors to trim photocopies as desired. Cut pieces from scrapbook paper to fit on cards and envelopes. Using spray adhesive, layer and glue photocopies and scrapbook paper on cards and envelopes.

Instead of buying flannel-backed vinyl by the yard for your Sit-Upon, you can use a vinyl tablecloth.

## 1 No-Sew Table Runner
*(shown on page 53)*

You will need 2¹/₈ yds red and white striped fabric, ⁷/₈"w fusible web tape, 1¹/₄ yds of 1"w blue pom-pom fringe, and fabric glue.

*Yardage is based on fabric with a 40" usable width.*
Cut a 22" x 75" piece from fabric. Fuse web tape along long edges on wrong side of fabric; fuse edges 1" to wrong side. Cut two 21¹/₄" lengths of fringe. Wrapping ends of fringe to back, glue fringe across ends of fabric piece; trim excess fringe.

## 2 No-Sew Tablecloth
*(shown on page 55)*

You will need a thumbtack, string, fabric marking pen, 44" square of red and white striped fabric, fabric glue, and 3⁷/₈ yds of 1"w blue pom-pom fringe.

*Our tablecloth was made to fit a 30" dia. tabletop. You may need to adjust measurements to fit your table.*
Follow **Cutting a Fabric Circle**, page 168, and use a 21¹/₂" measurement for string to mark, then cut a 43" dia. circle from fabric square. Glue fringe along edge on right side of fabric circle; trim excess fringe.

## 3 Sit-Upon
*(shown on page 54)*

You will need several folded newspaper sections (ours measure approximately 13¹/₂"w x 11¹/₂"h x ¹/₂"-thick), red gingham flannel-backed vinyl, stapler, fabric glue, ¹/₂"w blue rickrack, and pinking shears.

Unfold newspaper sections and measure width and height; cut a piece from vinyl 3" larger than width and 4" larger than height. Matching wrong sides and short edges, fold vinyl in half. Matching folds, place newspaper between vinyl layers. Staple through both vinyl layers just outside newspaper along open edges. Wrapping ends to back at folded edge, glue rickrack over staples. Use pinking shears to trim vinyl edges to ¹/₂" outside rickrack.

## 4 Firecracker Favors
*(shown on page 55)*

To make 10 favors, you will need 5 paper towel tubes; ⁵/₈ yd red and white striped fabric; pinking shears; fabric glue; 1⁵/₈ yds of 1¹/₂"w red, white, and blue striped ribbon; individually wrapped candies; red, white, and blue star sprays; and blue tinsel stems.

*Yardage is based on fabric with a 40" usable width.*
1. Cut tubes in half. For each favor, cut a 5³/₄" x 10" piece from fabric. Pink one end of fabric piece for top of favor. Centering tube on one long edge of fabric and overlapping and gluing ends at back, cover tube with fabric. Gather and glue bottom end of fabric closed. Tuck glued end into tube.
2. Overlapping ends at back, glue a ribbon length around favor.
3. Place candies, then a star spray inside favor. Gather fabric around spray at top of favor and secure with a tinsel stem; wrap ends of stem around a pencil to curl.

## 5 Personalized Plate Wreath
*(shown on page 59)*

You will need a hot glue gun, tuna can, 9" dia. white pierced-edge plate, assorted ribbons, 14" dia. artificial greenery wreath, silk daisies, and a dry-erase marker.

*Use caution when working with glue gun.*
1. Hot glue can to center back of plate (this will stabilize the plate against the door or wall).
2. Use ribbon to tie plate to wreath.
3. Remove daisies from stems; hot glue daisies to wreath.
4. Tie ribbons into a bow. Hot glue bow to wreath. Write message on plate with dry-erase marker.

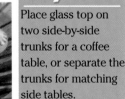

## 6 Water Hose Wreath
*(shown on page 58)*

You will need a green water hose, floral wire, wire cutters, 5"h x 4½" dia. watering can, hot glue gun, floral swag, and raffia.

*Use caution when working with glue gun.* Shape six loops of hose into a 19" dia. wreath; cut off excess hose. For top of wreath, wire loops together tightly at one end. Attach handle of watering can to top of wreath with floral wire. Wire swag to top of wreath, securing with hot glue as needed. Tie raffia into a bow; attach to wreath at top of swag with floral wire.

## 7 Gift Bags
*(shown on page 62)*

To make 10 gift bags, you will need ⅝"w fusible web tape, 1⅛ yds black and white toile fabric, pinking shears, 10 cellophane bags, Flavored Sugar (recipe on page 62), twist ties, white cardstock, ⅛" dia. hole punch, black embroidery floss, 7 yds of ⅝"w black and white checked ribbon, hot glue gun, and large silk roses and leaves removed from stems.

*Yardage is based on fabric with a 40" usable width. Use caution when working with glue gun.*
1. For each bag, cut a 9¾" x 10½" piece from fabric. Fuse web tape along right side of one short edge of fabric piece. Matching right sides, fuse short edges together to make a tube. Flatten tube with seam at center back; press seam allowance to one side.
2. For bag bottom, fuse web tape along right side on one end of bag front; fuse bottom of bag closed. Turn bag right side out; pink top edge.
3. Fill cellophane bag with Flavored Sugar, then seal bag with twist tie. Place cellophane bag in gift bag.

4. Photocopy recipe tag, page 170, onto cardstock; cut out. Punch a hole in corner of tag. Thread a length of floss through hole; knot ends together. Thread tag onto a 25" length of ribbon. Gathering top of bag, knot ribbon around bag. Tie ends into a bow; trim and notch ends. Hot glue rose and leaves to bag front.

## 8 Flower Patch Quilt
*(shown on page 65)*

You will need twenty 13" squares of assorted print fabrics, 1⅞ yds of 60"w fabric for backing and binding, 12 assorted buttons, and embroidery floss.

*Match right sides and use a ½" seam allowance for all sewing.*
1. For quilt front, sew four 13" squares together to make a 49" long strip; repeat to make a total of five strips. Matching seams, sew long edges of strips together.
2. For backing, cut a 52" x 64" piece from fabric. Matching wrong sides and with 1½" extended past each edge of quilt front, pin backing to front. For binding, press top and bottom edges of backing ¾" to wrong side twice, overlapping edges of quilt front; repeat with side edges. Sew along inside edges of binding on quilt front.
3. Knotting and leaving floss ends long at front of button, use floss to sew a button to quilt front at each intersection where corners of fabric squares meet.

## 9 Wicker End Table
*(shown on page 64)*

You will need a round white wicker table (ours has a 24" dia. removable tabletop with an 18¼" dia. inset); painter's masking tape; green and pink spray paint; clear acrylic spray sealer; poster board, floral fabric, and paper-backed fusible web (optional); and a round, polished-edged piece of glass for tabletop.

*tip* — Place glass top on two side-by-side trunks for a coffee table, or separate the trunks for matching side tables.

*Use spray paint and sealer in a well-ventilated area. Allow paint and sealer to dry after each application.*

1. Remove tabletop from table. Masking as necessary, paint tabletop green and pink as desired; apply sealer.
2. If your tabletop has an inset area, cut a circle from poster board to fit inset. Cut a circle from fabric and fusible web $^3/_4$" larger all around than poster board circle. Fuse web circle to wrong side of fabric circle; remove paper backing. Clipping curves and fusing edges to back of poster board, fuse fabric circle to poster board circle.
3. Reassemble table; place covered poster board in inset. Place glass on table.

## 10 Floral Pillow
*(shown on page 64)*

You will need $^1/_2$ yd floral fabric, $^1/_4$ yd green/white ticking, 12" square pillow form, fabric glue, $1^1/_2$ yds white chenille rickrack, and six 1" dia. flower buttons.

*Yardages are based on fabric with a 40" usable width. Match right sides and use a $^1/_2$" seam allowance for all sewing.*

1. For pillow front and back, cut two 13" squares from floral fabric and four 4" x 13" strips from ticking. Sew a ticking strip to opposite sides of each floral square; press seam allowance open.
2. Leaving one end open, sew pillow front and back together. Clip corners and turn right side out. Sewing through pillow front and back, sew over seam between ticking and floral fabric on finished end of pillow. Insert pillow form. Sew over remaining seam between ticking and floral fabric, then sew opening closed.
3. Matching ends at back, glue rickrack to pillow over seams. Starting 3" from one end of each ticking piece, sew three buttons, 3" apart, to ticking on pillow front.

## 11 Placecard Flowerpots
*(shown on page 66)*

For each placecard, you will need a 4"h x 3" dia. terra-cotta flowerpot, white acrylic paint, paintbrushes, black chalkboard paint, craft glue, $9^1/_2$" length of trim, chalk, and a candle to fit in pot.

*Allow paint to dry after each application. Never leave burning candles unattended.*

Paint pot white. Paint bottom of pot with chalkboard paint. Glue trim around rim of pot. Write name on pot with chalk; place candle in pot.

## 12 Hanging Lantern
*(shown on page 66)*

You will need removable tape; hanging lantern with glass cover (our cover is 6"w x $10^1/_2$"h x $5^3/_4$"d); black liquid leading paint; leading tip set; purple, blue, dark yellow, yellow, green, red, and white glass paints; and a liner brush and other paintbrushes.

*Follow instructions on glass paint to determine the need for glass conditioner and for finishing and drying instructions.*

1. Use a photocopier to enlarge design, page 170, to 128%; cut out. Center and tape design, with right side toward glass, to inside of cover front.
2. Attach leading tip to leading bottle. Apply thin lines of leading over design outlines; allow to dry overnight.
3. Fill in the leaded areas with glass paints. Make sure paint connects to leading lines, using liner brush if needed. Blend colors together on glass while wet for shading and highlighting.

## 13 Floating Candles
*(shown on page 67)*

You will need candle painting medium; green, yellow, pink, and orange acrylic paints; paintbrushes; and 3" dia. round floating candles.

*Never leave burning candles unattended.*

Mix equal parts candle medium and paint for each color. Use a flat brush to paint border around top of candle. Use end of paintbrush handle to make dots on top of candle.

## 14 Storage Trunk Coffee Table
*(shown on page 70)*

You will need two trunks (ours measure 19"w x 20"h x $15^1/_2$"d), dark ecru acrylic paint, antiquing gel, paintbrushes, soft cloth, fabric, spray adhesive, hot glue gun, and a large piece of glass with polished edges for tabletop.

*Use adhesive in a well-ventilated area. Use caution when working with glue gun.*

Carefully remove latch and trim from front panel of each trunk. Paint center of lid dark ecru; allow to dry. Dry brush antiquing gel over paint, then wipe surface with cloth. Cut a piece of fabric to fit front panel. Use spray adhesive to glue fabric to panel. Replace latch; hot glue trim back in place over fabric edges. Arrange trunks as desired, then place tabletop on top of trunks.

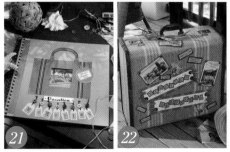

## 15 Multi-Tiered Fountain
*(shown on page 71)*

You will need paintbrushes, waterproof sealer, 7$^1/_2$"h x 10" dia. cast iron urn with handles, 7"h x 6$^1/_4$" dia. cast iron urn with at least a $^1/_2$" dia. hole in bottom, cast iron bird to fit in small urn, polished stones, tabletop fountain pump kit to fit under base of small urn, 7" length of $^1/_2$" dia. plastic tubing, and silicone adhesive.

Seal inside and outside of urns and bird. Place some stones and fountain pump in large urn. Attach tubing to pump. Running tubing through hole in bottom of small urn, arrange small urn over pump. Fill in around bottom of small urn with stones. Seal hole around tubing with silicone adhesive and allow to dry. Holding tubing upright, fill small urn with stones. Trim tubing in small urn to desired length. Arrange bird over tubing in small urn. Follow manufacturer's instructions to add water and operate pump.

## 16 Magazine Basket
*(shown on page 70)*

You will need a woven basket, fabric, hot glue gun, and decorative trim.

*Use caution when working with glue gun.*
1. Measure around basket; add 2$^1/_2$". Measure from where you want fabric to begin at top of basket to bottom of basket; add 1$^1/_2$". Cut a piece from fabric the determined measurements.
2. Baste along bottom edge of fabric piece. Press, then glue one side edge of fabric 1" to wrong side. Overlapping and gluing side edges at back and gluing top edge of fabric to basket, cover basket with fabric.
3. Pull basting stitches to gather fabric tightly around bottom of basket; knot and trim thread, then spot glue fabric to basket bottom.
4. Glue trim along top edge of fabric.

## 17 Gardener's Mailbox
*(shown on page 72)*

You will need spray primer; metal rural mailbox; yellow, khaki, and green spray paints; painter's masking tape; and matte clear acrylic spray sealer.

*Use spray primer, paint, and sealer in a well-ventilated area. Allow primer, paint, and sealer to dry after each application.*
Prime mailbox; paint yellow. Wrapping tape completely around mailbox, mask mailbox as desired, then paint mailbox khaki; remove tape. Mask again and apply green paint. Apply sealer to mailbox.

## 18 Wind Chimes
*(shown on page 73)*

You will need needle-nose pliers, serving fork and five other assorted pieces of silverware, hammer and nail, block of wood, safety goggles, drill with metal bit, clear fishing line, and assorted beads.

*Wear safety goggles when operating drill.*
1. Use pliers to curl tines of serving fork. Determine arrangement of fork and silverware. Use hammer and nail to make six indentations along serving fork handle and one in the end of each handle on silverware pieces. Place serving fork and silverware pieces on wood block and drill a hole at each indentation.
2. For hanger, cut two 30" lengths of fishing line. Fold each length in half. Use a lark's head knot (**Fig. 1**) to secure one length through hole at end of serving fork handle and other length around end tine of fork. Knot lengths together 7$^1/_2$" from fork. Thread beads onto both lengths; knot ends.

**Fig. 1**

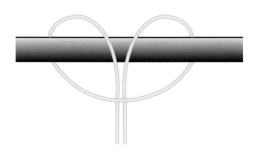

3. To attach silverware to fork, cut five 8" lengths of fishing line. Thread a silverware piece to center of each line length; with ends together, thread beads onto line. Knot line ends through a hole in fork.

## 19 Water Gun Bin
*(shown on page 73)*

You will need a white metal bin with lid (ours is 12"w x 12"h x 8¹/₂"d), paper-backed fusible vinyl, spray adhesive, and foam flower and dot stickers.

*Use adhesive in a well-ventilated area.* Use a photocopier to enlarge design, page 171, to 112%. Remove paper backing from vinyl. Place vinyl, adhesive side down, on design. Smooth with fingers to remove air bubbles. Using paper backing as a pressing cloth, fuse vinyl to design; cut out design ¹/₈" from edges. Use spray adhesive to glue design to front of bin. Adhere stickers to front of bin.

## 20 Straw Tote and Gardening Gloves
*(shown on page 73)*

You will need three 3¹/₂" dia. and two 2" dia. pale yellow silk flowers; straw tote bag; three 1¹/₄" dia. and two ⁷/₈" dia. brown buttons; green thread; and green, khaki, and yellow striped garden gloves.

Remove flowers from stems. For tote, spacing flowers evenly and sewing through flower and bag, sew a large button to center of each large flower to attach flowers to bag. Sewing through flower and glove, sew a small button to center of each small flower to attach a flower to center of each glove cuff.

## 21 Vacation Scrapbook
*(shown on page 76)*

You will need lizard skin print scrapbook paper, acid-free glue, a 12" x 12" spiral-bound album with 3" square opening in cover, two 5¹/₂" lengths of ⁵/₈"w brown striped ribbon, tan cardstock, fine-point permanent pen, two ¹/₈" dia. silver brads, metal "Vacation" scrapbook tag with holes in ends, ¹/₈" dia. hole punch, brown embroidery floss, assorted brown and tan buttons, and a postcard.

1. For suitcase, cut a 5¹/₂" x 8" piece from scrapbook paper; center and glue on album front. Cut an X in paper over opening. Fold and glue paper to inside cover. Center and glue a ribbon length between opening and each side edge of suitcase.
2. Make a color photocopy of designs on page 172; cut out. Glue border to album front along binding. Glue handle and corners to suitcase. Cut out opening in tag. Glue tag to cardstock; cut out just outside tag edge. Write message on cardstock in tag opening. Glue tag to suitcase.
3. Attach brads in holes in metal tag; center and glue tag below suitcase. Glue photocopied letters to cardstock. Cut cardstock into a tag around each letter. Punch a hole in top of each tag. For each tag, knot ends of a 4" length of floss together. Knot looped end of floss through hole in tag. Arrange and glue letter tags below metal tag. Glue a button to album over floss of each tag.
4. Glue postcard to inside front cover behind opening.

## 22 Vacation Keepsake Valise
*(shown on page 77)*

You will need a 12" x 12" sheet of handwriting scrapbook paper, one 8¹/₂" x 11" sheet each of two coordinating papers, pinking shears, ¹/₈ yd coordinating fabric, craft glue, brown cardstock, green raffia, eight assorted buttons, vintage suitcase, two 3¹/₂" x 5¹/₂" postcards, scraps of faux leather, and silk flowers, removed from stems.

*Yardage is based on fabric with a 40" usable width.*

1. Make a color photocopy of designs on page 171; cut out.
2. Cut two 2¹/₂" x 12" strips from 12" x 12" paper. Using pinking shears on long edges, cut a 3¹/₂" x 13" and a 3¹/₂" x 13³/₄" strip from fabric. Arrange and glue letters on paper strips. With "VACATION" strip on short fabric strip, center and glue paper strips on fabric strips. Leaving ends long, knot lengths of raffia through buttons. Glue a button to each corner of paper strips. Arrange and glue fabric strips on suitcase.
3. Cut a 4" x 6" piece from each 8¹/₂" x 11" paper. Center and glue a postcard on each paper piece. Glue photo corners to postcard corners; glue postcards to suitcase.
4. Glue sayings to faux leather; cut out. Randomly glue leather pieces to suitcase.
5. Glue flowers to suitcase. Tie raffia into a bow around suitcase handle.

*tip*

To save cardstock on the Pumpkin Seed Favors, print or write "toasted pumpkin seeds" several times on one sheet. Be sure to leave plenty of room to cut cardstock into tags.

## 1 No-Sew Table Throw
*(shown on page 80)*

You will need 1$^1$/$_2$ yds of 54"w fabric, 6$^1$/$_8$ yds tassel trim, and a hot glue gun.

*Use caution when working with glue gun.* If necessary, square up fabric piece. Gently bending trim around corners, hot glue trim along all edges of fabric; overlap ends, then cut off excess trim.

## 2 Pumpkin Seed Favors
*(shown on page 86)*

To make 10 favors, you will need a hot glue gun, 10 small brown paper bags (we used penny-sacks, which are commonly found at hardware stores), craft glue, decorative-edged craft scissors, white cardstock, $^1$/$_4$" dia. hole punch, 10 cellophane bags, Toasted Pumpkin Seeds (recipe on page 87), twist ties, orange raffia, and 10 silk leaves.

*Use caution when working with glue gun.*
1. For each favor, hot glue bottom fold of bag to back to flatten bag. Make a color photocopy of design on page 161; cut out. Use craft glue to adhere design to bag front $^1$/$_2$" from bottom edge. Trim top edge of bag with craft scissors.
2. Print or write "toasted pumpkin seeds" on cardstock; cut into a 1" x 3$^1$/$_2$" tag. Punch a hole in end of tag.
3. Fill cellophane bag with $^1$/$_2$ cup of pumpkin seeds; seal with twist tie. Place cellophane bag in paper bag, then fold top of bag down 1$^1$/$_4$". Punch two holes, $^3$/$_4$" apart, through folded section at center top of bag. Thread raffia ends through holes from back to front; knot at front. Thread tag onto raffia. Tie raffia into a bow. Hot glue leaf to top flap of bag.

## 3 Apple Wreath
*(shown on page 91)*

You will need an artificial berry garland, 19" dia. grapevine wreath, floral wire, wire cutters, hot glue gun, ball point pen or awl, artificial apples, floral picks, and silk leaves.

*Use caution when working with glue gun.* Arrange garland on wreath; attach garland to wreath with floral wire, hot gluing to secure as needed. Use pen to make a hole in each apple. Hot glue flat end of a floral pick in hole. Insert picks in wreath, hot gluing apples to wreath as needed. Hot glue leaves to wreath.

## 4 Autumn Angel
*(shown on page 92)*

You will need $^3$/$_4$ yd gold plaid fabric, 1"w fusible web tape, standard white eyelet pillowcase, gold and white embroidery floss, 12$^1$/$_4$"-long oversized wooden spoon, hot glue gun, white 12" x 18" fabric place mat with decorative edges, 40" length of wired fall garland, wire cutters, large silk flower for hair, silk leaves, artificial berries, 1 yd of $^5$/$_8$"w sheer gold ribbon, dark brown water-based wood stain, two 6$^1$/$_8$" x 8$^5$/$_8$" gingerbread brackets, soft cloth, white and cream acrylic paints, paintbrushes, matte clear acrylic sealer, wood glue, 5" square wooden plaque, 3"w x 6"h x 1"-thick block of wood, 2$^3$/$_4$" dia. artificial pumpkin, and a small plate hanger.

*Yardage is based on fabric with a 40" usable width. Use caution when working with glue gun. Allow paint and sealer to dry after each application.*
1. Cut a 37$^1$/$_2$" x 24$^1$/$_2$" piece from plaid fabric. Fuse web tape along one long edge; fuse edge 1$^1$/$_4$" to wrong side. Press opposite edge 1$^1$/$_4$" to wrong side.
2. Cut pillowcase open at center back. Cutting excess from center back and sewn bottom end, cut a 35$^1$/$_2$" x 19$^3$/$_4$" piece from pillowcase; press long raw edge 1$^1$/$_4$" to wrong side.
3. Follow **Embroidery**, page 169, to sew running stitches along center of pressed edge of fabric with gold floss and center of pressed edge of pillowcase with white floss. With raw edges at back of spoon (concave side) and hot gluing in spots to secure, pull stitches in fabric to gather fabric around spoon handle $^1$/$_2$" below bowl of spoon; knot and trim floss. Arrange pillowcase over fabric. Hot gluing in spots, pull stitches in pillowcase to gather edge of pillowcase above gathered edge of fabric; knot and trim floss.

4. For sleeves, matching wrong sides and long edges, fold place mat in half. At each end of open long edge, glue 4" of edge closed. Cut a 2" long neck opening at center of folded edge. For back, cutting through one layer only, cut an opening in one side from bottom of mat to neck opening (**Fig. 1**).

**Fig. 1**

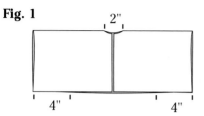

5. Remove pieces from 6" of wire at each end of garland. Thread one end of garland through each opening at ends of place mat. Twist garland ends together at back of "neck." Overlapping edges at back as necessary, arrange place mat around "neck;" hot glue edges together at back. Shape place mat around garland for arms.

6. Gluing several petals to the front for bangs, hot glue flower to spoon. Arrange, then hot glue several leaves on back of flower and berries on front of flower. Tie ribbon into a bow around "neck;" trim ends. Tuck stems of a few leaves under ribbon; hot glue to secure.

7. Stain brackets; wipe away excess with a soft cloth, then allow to dry. Dry brush brackets with white and cream paints, then apply sealer.

8. Follow **Fig. 2** and **Fig. 3** and use wood glue to assemble wooden pieces.

**Fig. 2**

**Fig. 3**

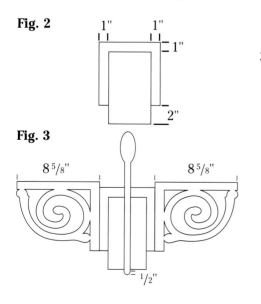

9. Hot glue pumpkin to garland. Attach plate hanger to back of wooden plaque.

## 5 Painted Bureau
*(shown on page 90)*

You will need a small two-drawer chest; sandpaper; four large round wooden finials (and hardware) for feet; spray primer; gold, green, purple, and red spray paint; $^3/_4$"w and $1^1/_2$"w painter's masking tape; walnut gel stain; soft cloth; spray polyurethane finish; leaf drawer pulls; floral foam to fit in bottom drawer; and artificial pumpkins, gourds, leaves, berries, and flowers.

*Use spray primer, paint, and finish in a well-ventilated area. Allow primer, paint, and finish to dry after each application.*

1. Remove knobs, hardware, and drawers from chest. Sand, then prime chest, drawer fronts, and finials. Paint chest and finials gold and drawer fronts green. Use $^3/_4$"w tape to mask off a border along edges on top of chest. Paint top purple; remove tape. Attach finials to bottom of legs.

2. For stripes on each drawer front, mark center of drawer, then center a piece of $1^1/_2$"w tape down front of drawer over mark. Continue adhering pieces of $1^1/_2$"w tape at each side of center piece until drawer front is covered with tape. Working from center outward, remove every other piece of tape, then paint drawer front red. Once paint is dry, remove remaining tape. Apply stain to chest and drawer fronts. While stain is wet, wipe away excess with soft cloth. Apply several coats of finish to chest and drawers.

3. Attach leaf drawer pulls to drawers. Replace drawers in chest. Arrange floral foam, then pumpkins, gourds, leaves, berries, and flowers in bottom drawer.

## 6 Gift Cones
*(shown on page 94)*

To make 10 cones, you will need tracing paper, $^3/_4$ yd of 54"w upholstery fabric, hot glue gun, 4 yds jute twine, silk leaves, Sugared Maple Pecans (recipe on page 94), 10 cellophane bags, twist ties, $4^3/_4$ yds of $^1/_8$"w ribbon, and ten $1^1/_2$" dia. round tags.

*Use caution when working with glue gun.* Trace cone pattern, page 173, onto tracing paper; cut out. Using tracing paper pattern, cut 10 cone pieces from fabric. Overlapping sides approximately 2" at top, roll each piece into a cone; glue edges together at seam. Flatten cone with seam at center back. Knot each end of a 14" length of jute; glue a knot on each side of cone. Glue leaves to front of cone. Place pecans in a cellophane bag; seal with a twist tie. Knot a 17" ribbon length around cellophane bag. Write a message on a tag. Thread tag onto one ribbon end, then tie ribbon into a bow. Place gift in cone.

## 7 Pinecone Fire Starters
*(shown on page 96)*

You will need scented candles, a 3-pound coffee can, electric skillet, scented oil, dried pinecones, floral wire, wire cutters, and newspaper.

*Use caution when working with hot wax and when burning Fire Starters.* Melt candles in coffee can placed in electric skillet filled with water. Add drops of oil to melted candles. To make a hanger for dipping pinecones, wrap floral wire around bottom of each pinecone; form a hook in opposite end of wire. Dip pinecones into melted candles several times, allowing wax to harden after each dip. Covering surface beneath pinecones with newspaper, hang pinecones to harden completely. Carefully remove hangers from pinecones.

*tip* Cut several cardboard inserts to fit any tray. Cover with fabric to match décor for any season or party theme.

## 8 Fabric-Covered Pots
*(shown on page 96)*

You will need clay pots (we used 7$\frac{1}{2}$"h x 6$\frac{1}{4}$" dia. and 9$\frac{1}{4}$"h x 8$\frac{1}{4}$" dia. pots), flannel shirts, rubber bands, and a hot glue gun.

*Use caution when working with glue gun.* For each pot, cut a circle from the back of a flannel shirt. Select a pot to fit circle by setting pot at center of circle and gathering fabric around pot at top. Secure fabric at rim with a rubber band. Folding edge of fabric 1" to wrong side, adjust gathers and hot glue fabric to pot along top edge; remove rubber band. Cut button placket from shirt; hot glue placket around pot.

## 9 Autumn Leaves Washtub
*(shown on page 98)*

You will need a black metal washtub with handles, cream acrylic paint, 1" square sponge, silk leaves, craft glue, and clear acrylic spray sealer.

*Use sealer in a well-ventilated area.* Beginning at center of each side of tub and working toward the handles, sponge checkerboard pattern along top edge of tub with cream paint. Remove veins and stems from leaves. Place a blank piece of paper over leaves; press leaves. Glue leaves to tub as desired. Apply sealer to tub.

## 10 Fabric-Lined Tray
*(shown on page 99)*

You will need cardboard, a serving tray, fabric, paper-backed fusible web, and a hot glue gun.

*Use caution when working with glue gun.* Cut a piece of cardboard to fit inside tray. Cut a piece from fabric and fusible web $\frac{1}{2}$" larger on all sides than cardboard piece. Fuse web to fabric; remove paper backing. Wrapping edges to back and hot gluing at corners to secure, fuse fabric to cardboard. Place covered cardboard in tray.

## 11 Mug Cozies
*(shown on page 99)*

For each mug cozy, you will need a mug, pinking shears, quilted fabric, $\frac{7}{8}$"w fusible web tape, embroidery floss, and four $\frac{5}{8}$" dia. buttons.

Measure around mug. Use pinking shears to cut a 3$\frac{1}{4}$"w fabric piece 1" longer than the determined measurement. Fuse web tape along wrong side of each end; fuse ends 1" to wrong side. Center and use floss to sew two buttons $\frac{1}{2}$" apart on each end of fabric piece. Cut a 22" length of floss; knot each end. With ends at sides of handle, wrap warmer around mug. Wrap floss around buttons in a figure-8 pattern, then tie ends into a bow at top of handle.

## 12 Pumpkin Fountain
*(shown on page 99)*

You will need waterproof sealer, a paintbrush, tabletop fountain pump kit, large glass bowl, $\frac{1}{2}$" dia. plastic tubing, hollow metal pumpkin with small opening at top for tubing and opening at bottom large enough to fit over pump, 20-gauge wire, wire cutters, and polished stones.

Seal entire pumpkin. Place pump in bowl; attach tubing. Place pumpkin in bowl over pump and tubing. Trim tubing to fit to top of pumpkin; secure with wire if necessary (our tubing fit inside the coiled wire at the top of our pumpkin). Arrange stones in bowl around pumpkin. Follow pump manufacturer's instructions to add water and operate pump.

## 13 Gourd Birdhouse
*(shown on page 100)*

You will need a drill with a small bit and 2" dia. hole-saw attachment, dried gourd, sandpaper, orange and black acrylic paints, paintbrushes, 1$\frac{1}{4}$" dia. round foam brush, clear acrylic sealer, 18-gauge copper wire, wire cutters, and needle-nose pliers.

*Allow paint and sealer to dry after each application.*

Use hole-saw attachment to drill an opening in gourd; sand opening. For hanger, use small bit to drill two holes in top of gourd. Mix equal parts water and orange paint; paint gourd. Use foam brush to paint black dots on gourd; apply sealer. Thread gourd onto center of a 27" length of wire. Bend wire ends into a hanging loop, twisting wire tightly around itself to secure.

## 14 Punched Tin Lantern
*(shown on page 100)*

You will need a $4^3/_4$"h x 4" dia. can, towel, hammer and nail or awl, spray primer, orange spray paint, dark brown gel stain, soft cloth, clear acrylic spray sealer, brown embroidery floss, assorted buttons, $13^1/_2$" length of $^7/_8$"w orange grosgrain ribbon, craft glue, two 14" lengths of 24-gauge wire, needle-nose pliers, wire cutters, 1" dia. button, and a candle to fit in can.

*Use spray primer, paint, and sealer in a well-ventilated area. Allow primer, paint, and sealer to dry after each application. Never leave burning candles unattended.*

1. Fill can with water; freeze. Place can on towel; use hammer and nail or awl to punch two rows of holes around can 1" from top and bottom edges. Punch a hole in each side of can for hanger.
2. Empty and dry can thoroughly. Prime, then paint can orange. Apply stain; wipe off excess with cloth and allow to dry. Apply sealer.
3. Use floss to sew assorted buttons along center of ribbon length. Overlapping ends, glue ribbon length around center of can.
4. For hanger, thread one end of a wire length through hole in each side of can. Twist wire around itself for $1^1/_2$". Thread 1" dia. button onto remaining end of both wire lengths. Twist wire together above button; trim excess wire. Place candle in can.

## 15 Happy Halloween Table with Chairs
*(shown on page 101)*

You will need painter's masking tape, wax paper, black wooden bistro set, orange spray paint, clear acrylic spray sealer, two orange and black checked dish towels (we used 16" x 29" towels), 1" thick foam to fit each chair seat, black and orange embroidery floss, pinking shears, $3^7/_8$ yds of $^7/_8$"w orange grosgrain ribbon, and four 1" dia. black buttons.

*Use spray paint and sealer in a well-ventilated area.*

1. Overlapping edges, adhere strips of tape to wax paper until you have a large enough sheet to draw face patterns on. Freehand draw patterns on tape sheet; cut out and remove wax paper. Pressing edges down firmly, arrange and adhere patterns on tabletop. Paint tabletop orange. Allow to dry, then remove patterns. Apply sealer.
2. For each cushion, fold towel over foam piece. Using six strands of black floss, follow **Embroidery**, page 169, to sew running stitches next to foam along open edges of towel. Pink edges of towel.
3. For ties, fold 34" lengths of ribbon in half. Sewing through ribbon and cushion, use six strands of orange floss to sew a button over folded end of ribbon at back corners of cushion.

## 16 Candy Corn Pillows
*(shown on page 102)*

For each pillow, you will need freezer paper; $^1/_8$ yd white, $^1/_4$ yd orange, and $^1/_4$ yd yellow fleece; black embroidery floss; and polyester fiberfill.

Trace top pattern, page 174, onto dull side of freezer paper twice; cut out. Matching shiny sides, fold a piece of freezer paper in half. Aligning patterns along fold as indicated, trace middle and bottom patterns twice each onto dull side of paper; cut out and unfold patterns. Iron shiny side of freezer paper patterns to wrong side of appropriate fleece colors; cut out.

Remove freezer paper. For each side of pillow, matching right sides and using a $^1/_2$" seam allowance, sew one top, middle, and bottom piece together. Matching wrong sides, place pillow front and back together. Leaving an opening for stuffing, follow **Embroidery**, page 169, to blanket stitch front and back together with six strands of floss. Insert fiberfill, then blanket stitch opening closed.

## 17 Mr. Scarecrow Pillow
*(shown on page 102)*

You will need a $24^1/_2$" x $28^1/_2$" piece of burlap, 1"w fusible web tape, scrap of orange felt, two $1^1/_4$" dia. buttons, red and white acrylic paints, paintbrushes, fabric glue, black jumbo rickrack, black embroidery floss, polyester fiberfill, rubber band, hot glue gun, artificial leaves and sunflower, and a straw hat.

*Use caution when working with glue gun.*

1. For hair, fray 5" of one long edge of burlap. Starting below hair, fuse web tape along right side of one short edge of fabric piece. Matching right sides, fuse short edges together to make a tube. Flatten tube with seam at center back; press seam to one side.
2. For bottom of pillow, fuse web tape along right side on bottom end of pillow front; fuse bottom of pillow closed. Turn pillow right side out.
3. Cut a nose from felt. Refer to photo to sew buttons to pillow front for eyes, add cheeks with red paint, and glue nose and rickrack mouth in place with fabric glue. Add highlights to eyes with white paint. Follow **Embroidery**, page 169, to sew straight stitches over mouth with six strands of floss.
4. Fill pillow with fiberfill; gather top of pillow with rubber band. Hot glue leaves and flower to hat. Arrange hair, then hot glue hat on head.

## 18 Alda's Autumn Afghan
*(shown on page 103)*

Finished Size: 54" x 66" (137 cm x 168 cm)

*Read Knit and Crochet Basics, pages 168 – 169, before beginning Afghan.*

### Materials

Worsted Weight Yarn: **MEDIUM 4**
- [6 ounces, 330 yards (170 grams, 300 meters) per skein]
  Cream - 7 skeins
- [6 ounces, 326 yards (170 grams, 298 meters) per skein]
  Lt Brown - 2 skeins
  Brown and Rust - 1 skein each
- [5 ounces, 277 yards (141 grams, 253 meters) per skein]
  Red - 1 skein
- [8 ounces, 452 yards (226 grams, 413 meters) per skein]
  Gold - 1 skein

Crochet hook, size J (6 mm) **or** size needed for gauge

Yarn needle

**Gauge Swatch:** Each Square = 3" (7.5 cm). Work same as Square A.

Referring to the **Key**, page 159, make the number of squares specified in the colors indicated.

### Square A

With color indicated, ch 4; join with slip st to form a ring.

**Rnd 1** (Right side)**:** Ch 3 **(counts as first dc, now and throughout)**, 2 dc in ring, ch 2, (3 dc in ring, ch 2) 3 times; join with slip st to first dc: 12 dc and 4 ch-2 sps.

*Note:* Loop a short piece of yarn around any stitch to mark Rnd 1 as **right** side.

**Rnd 2:** Slip st in next 2 dc and in next ch-2 sp, ch 3, (2 dc, ch 2, 3 dc) in same sp, ch 1, ★ (3 dc, ch 2, 3 dc) in next ch-2 sp, ch 1; repeat from ★ 2 times **more**; join with slip st to first dc, finish off: 24 dc and 8 sps.

### Square B

With Cream, ch 4; join with slip st to form a ring.

**Rnd 1** (Right side)**:** Ch 5 **(counts as first dc plus ch 2)**, 3 dc in ring, cut Cream, with second color indicated, YO and draw through, ch 1, (3 dc, ch 2, 3 dc) in ring, cut second color, with Cream, YO and draw through, ch 1, 2 dc in ring; join with slip st to first dc: 12 dc and 4 ch-2 sps.

*Note:* Mark Rnd 1 as **right** side.

**Rnd 2:** Slip st in first ch-2 sp, ch 3, (2 dc, ch 2, 3 dc) in same sp, ch 1, 3 dc in next ch-2 sp, cut Cream, with second color, YO and draw through, ch 1, 3 dc in same sp, ch 1, (3 dc, ch 2, 3 dc) in next ch-2 sp, ch 1, 3 dc in next ch-2 sp, cut second color, with Cream, YO and draw through, ch 1, 3 dc in same sp, ch 1; join with slip st to first dc, finish off: 24 dc and 8 sps.

### Assembly

With matching color, using **Placement Diagram**, page 159, as a guide, and working through **inside** loops only, follow **Embroidery**, page 169, to whipstitch Squares together, forming 17 vertical strips of 21 Squares each, beginning in second ch of first corner ch-2 and ending in first ch of next corner ch-2; whipstitch strips together in same manner.

### Stems

*Note:* Keep working yarn to **wrong** side of Afghan.

With **right** side facing and Lt Brown, insert hook in corner of Square as indicated on **Placement Diagram** and pull up a loop, working diagonally, ★ insert hook in Square, YO and draw through **loosely** through loop on hook; repeat from ★ evenly spaced across to next corner; finish off.

Repeat for each Stem.

### Edging

**Rnd 1:** With **right** side facing, join Cream with sc in any corner ch-2 sp **(Joining With Sc, page 168)**; ch 2, sc in same sp, sc in each dc and in each sp and joining across to next corner ch-2 sp, ★ (sc, ch 2, sc) in corner ch-2 sp, sc in each dc and in each sp and joining across to next corner ch-2 sp; repeat from ★ 2 times **more**; join with slip st to first sc, finish off: 756 sc and 4 ch-2 sps.

**Rnd 2:** With **right** side facing, join Lt Brown with sc in any corner ch-2 sp; ch 2, sc in same sp, sc in each sc across to next corner ch-2 sp, ★ (sc, ch 2, sc) in corner ch-2 sp, sc in each sc across to next corner ch-2 sp; repeat from ★ 2 times **more**; join with slip st to first sc: 764 sc and 4 ch-2 sps.

**Rnd 3:** Slip st in first ch-2 sp, ch 5 **(counts as first hdc plus ch 3, now and**

**tip**
Alda's Autumn Afghan is a great take-along project since it is made one granny square at a time and then assembled. It could easily be adapted to a solid color afghan as well.

**throughout)**, hdc in same sp, ch 1, skip next sc, (hdc in next sc, ch 1, skip next sc) across to next corner ch-2 sp, ★ (hdc, ch 3, hdc) in corner ch-2 sp, ch 1, skip next sc, (hdc in next sc, ch 1, skip next sc) across to next corner ch-2 sp; repeat from ★ 2 times **more**; join with slip st to first hdc, finish off: 388 hdc and 388 sps.

**Rnd 4:** With **right** side facing, join Cream with sc in any corner ch-3 sp; ch 3, sc in same sp, ch 1, (sc in next ch-1 sp, ch 1) across to next corner ch-3 sp, ★ (sc, ch 3, sc) in corner ch-3 sp, ch 1, (sc in next ch-1 sp, ch 1) across to next corner ch-3 sp; repeat from ★ 2 times **more**; join with slip st to first sc, finish off: 392 sc and 392 sps.

**Rnd 5:** With **right** side facing, join Lt Brown with slip st in any corner ch-3 sp; ch 5, hdc in same sp, ch 1, ★ (hdc in next ch-1 sp, ch 1) across to next corner ch-3 sp, (hdc, ch 3, hdc) in corner ch-3 sp, ch 1; repeat from ★ 2 times **more**, (hdc in next ch-1 sp, ch 1) across; join with slip st to first hdc: 396 hdc and 396 sps.

**Rnd 6:** Slip st in next ch-3 sp, ch 1, sc in same sp, ch 3, (sc in next sp, ch 3) around; join with slip st to first sc, finish off.

**Design by Martha Brooks Stein**

### Placement Diagram

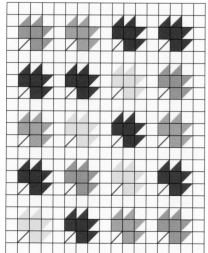

**Key**

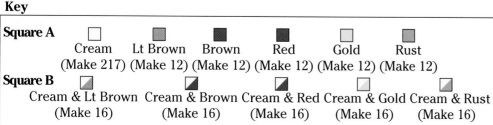

| Square A | | | | | |
|---|---|---|---|---|---|
| Cream | Lt Brown | Brown | Red | Gold | Rust |
| (Make 217) | (Make 12) | (Make 12) | (Make 12) | (Make 12) | (Make 12) |

| Square B | | | | |
|---|---|---|---|---|
| Cream & Lt Brown | Cream & Brown | Cream & Red | Cream & Gold | Cream & Rust |
| (Make 16) | (Make 16) | (Make 16) | (Make 16) | (Make 16) |

## 19 Crackled Bowl
*(shown on page 105)*

You will need primer; paintbrushes; wooden bowl; black, cranberry red, and green acrylic paints; crackle medium; sponge; 3 wooden drawer pulls; wood glue; and matte clear acrylic sealer.

*Allow paint and sealer to dry after each application. Bowl is not safe for use with food.*

Prime inside of bowl; paint inside of bowl black. Follow manufacturer's instructions to brush crackle medium on inside of bowl and sponge red paint over the crackled surface. Paint drawer pulls green; glue drawer pulls to bottom of bowl. Apply sealer to bowl.

## 20 Pumpkin Turkey
*(shown on page 106)*

You will need paper-backed fusible web, 1/4 yd each of orange fabric and muslin, 1/8 yd gold fabric, black and brown fabric scraps, three sheets of ecru felt, craft glue, nine 10" wooden skewers, white dimensional paint, poster board, two 3/8" dia. black shank buttons, 4" length of 5/8"w gold ribbon with sheer center, grapevine wreath with artificial leaves and berries, and a medium-size pumpkin.

1. Trace turkey head, beak, hat, and wattle, page 173, onto paper side of fusible web; cut out. Trace whole feather, feather top, and feather bottom nine times each onto paper side of fusible web; cut out. Fuse beak and feather bottoms to wrong side of orange fabric, whole feathers to wrong side of muslin, turkey head and feather tops to wrong side of gold fabric, and hat and wattle to wrong side of fabric scraps. Cut out all pieces; remove paper backing.
2. Overlapping each top and bottom 1/8", arrange feather tops and bottoms on felt; fuse in place. Cut feathers from felt.

3. Center and glue one skewer to felt side of each feather with pointed end of skewer extending 4" below bottom of feather. Fuse a muslin feather to back of each feather over skewer. Paint over raw fabric edges between each feather top and bottom with dimensional paint.
4. Cut a 4 1/2" x 8" rectangle from poster board. Arrange and fuse head and hat on poster board; cut out. Arrange and fuse beak and wattle appliqués on head. Sew buttons to head for eyes. Overlapping ends at back, glue ribbon length around hat for band. Remove a leaf from wreath and glue to hat.
5. Trim pumpkin stem flat; glue head to stem. Insert skewers into pumpkin. Place turkey on wreath.

## 21 Spider Candle Holders
*(shown on page 106)*

For each candle holder, you will need a hammer and nail or awl, tuna can, primer, paintbrushes, 1 1/2" dia. wooden drawer pull with one flat side, black metal paint, black and lime acrylic paints, clear acrylic sealer, craft glue, nine black chenille stems, hot glue gun, and a tea light.

*Allow primer, paint, and sealer to dry after each application. Use caution when working with glue gun. Never leave burning candles unattended.*

1. Use hammer and nail or awl to punch two holes 1" apart in center bottom of can.
2. Prime can and drawer pull. Paint entire can with metal paint. Paint drawer pull with black acrylic paint. Use end of paintbrush handle to paint lime dots on round side of drawer pull for eyes. Apply sealer to can and drawer pull. Glue drawer pull to can with craft glue.
3. For each pair of legs, twist two chenille stems together. Twisting ends together at bottom of can and trimming excess stem, form remaining chenille stem into a loop through holes in can. Thread legs through loop. Bend stem ends out for feet; arrange legs as desired. Hot glue centers of legs at bottom of can to secure. Place tea light in can.

Make color copies of favorite photos to use for your memory pages and keep the originals in a safe, dry place.

*tip*

## 22 Fred Scarecrow
*(shown on page 107)*

You will need two 6'-long and two 5'-long wooden garden stakes, hot glue gun, button-front shirt, medium-gauge wire, wire cutters, hammer and nails, blue jeans, two standard-size foam pillows, polyester fiberfill, suspenders, $24^1/_2$" x $28^1/_2$" piece of burlap, 1"w fusible web tape, rubber band, scrap of orange felt, two $1^1/_4$" dia. buttons, red and white acrylic paints, paintbrushes, fabric glue, black jumbo rickrack, black embroidery floss, bandanna, raffia, hat, vest, paper-backed fusible web, fabric scraps, artificial leaves and flowers, gloves, and rope.

*Use caution when working with glue gun.*

1. For base, stack and hot glue 6' stakes together. Repeat with 5' stakes for arms. Insert arms in sleeves of shirt. Leaving 6" of base at top, wire base and arms together to form a cross shape. Nail stakes together at intersection to secure.

2. Use a pencil to draw a line on jeans between top inner corners of back pockets. At center seam, cut an opening along drawn line for base to fit through. For legs, cut 6" of one end of a pillow in half. Place pillow in jeans with one half of cut end in each pants leg. Fill rest of legs with fiberfill. Place remaining pillow inside shirt for body; fill sleeves with fiberfill, then button shirt. Tucking shirt in jeans and inserting base through hole in back of jeans, pull jeans up over body. Attach suspenders to jeans.

3. For hair, fray 5" of one long edge of burlap. For head, starting below hair, fuse web tape along right side of one short edge of burlap piece. Matching right sides, fuse short edges together to make a tube. Flatten tube with seam at center back; press seam to one side. Turn right side out, then gather hair with rubber band.

4. Cut a nose from felt. Refer to photo to sew buttons to head for eyes, add cheeks with red paint, and glue nose and rickrack mouth in place with fabric glue. Add highlights to eyes with white paint. Follow **Embroidery**, page 169, to sew straight stitches over mouth with six strands of floss. Fill head with fiberfill. Place open end of head over top of base; secure with wire. Tie bandanna around neck of shirt. Cut raffia into desired lengths for straw (also cut enough for waist, arms, and legs and set aside). Hot glue straw along inside of shirt collar and pocket. Arrange hair, then hot glue hat on head.

5. For vest patches, fuse web to wrong side of fabric scraps. Cut fabric the desired sizes for patches; fuse patches to vest as desired. Slide one shoulder of vest over one arm. Cut other vest shoulder open; arrange vest on scarecrow. Hot glue leaves over cut edges.

6. Hot glue gloves and straw inside sleeve cuffs. Tie several lengths of raffia into a bow around each "wrist." Hot glue straw along inside of pants waist and legs. Knotting rope at front, thread a length of rope through belt loops; knot each end. Knot a length of rope around each "ankle."

7. Hot glue leaves and flowers to scarecrow as desired.

## 23 "Happy Fall" Scrapbook Page
*(shown on page 112)*

You will need one 12" x 12" sheet each of straw mat and denim scrapbook paper; acid-free glue; fine-point permanent pen; photographs; yellow, orange, and white cardstock; alphabet stickers; decorative-edged craft scissors (optional); $1/_4$" dia. hole punch; hole reinforcement; raffia; three silk leaves; and eight $1/_4$" dia. gold brads.

1. Cut wavy edges on straw mat paper; center and glue on denim paper. Draw "stitches" along edges of straw mat paper. Mat photos with yellow and orange cardstock; glue to page.

2. Make two color photocopies of pocket, page 170; cut out. Gluing along side and bottom edges only, glue pockets to page. Spell "HAPPY FALL" on orange cardstock with stickers; cut out and glue to one pocket. Cut a 2"w x 3³/₄"h tag from white cardstock. Punch a hole in tag; adhere reinforcement around hole. Write journaling on tag. Knot a length of raffia through hole in tag. Place tag in "HAPPY FALL" pocket.

3. Remove stems and veins from leaves. Place a piece of blank paper over leaves; press leaves. Glue one leaf to page at opening of plain pocket. Glue remaining leaves to page as desired. Glue raffia in plain pocket.

4. Attach brads to page at corners of straw mat paper and pockets.

## 24 Hayride Scrapbook Page
*(shown on page 112)*

You will need acid-free glue, 12" x 12" piece each of orange print scrapbook paper and poster board, 6" x 12" piece of green polka-dot scrapbook paper, 3¹/₂" x 12" piece of straw mat scrapbook paper, decorative-edged craft scissors, alphabet stickers, white cardstock, four ¹/₄" dia. gold brads, raffia, 6³/₄" x 9¹/₂" photograph, 7" x 9³/₄" piece of black cardstock, 24-gauge wire, wire cutters, hot glue gun, two ³/₄" dia. brown buttons, and an orange wooden frame with 3³/₄" x 5⁵/₈" opening.

*Use acid-free glue for all gluing unless otherwise indicated. Use caution when working with glue gun.*

1. Glue orange paper to poster board. Glue green paper along top edge of orange paper. Trim one long edge of straw mat paper with craft scissors; matching straight edges, glue straw mat paper along top edge of green paper.

2. Use craft scissors to cut a 1³/₄" x 10³/₄" strip from white cardstock. Adhere alphabet stickers to strip. Glue strip to center of straw mat paper; attach brads at corners of white strip. Wrap a length of raffia around brads. Knot ends at center bottom of strip; trim excess. Knot

several lengths of raffia together; trim ends to desired length. Glue in place over knot in first raffia length.

3. Center and glue photo on black cardstock; glue onto page. Cut a length of wire for frame hanger. Wrap ends of wire around a pencil to curl. Shape wire into a hanger, then hot glue wire above curls to frame. Knotting ends at front, thread a length of raffia through each button; trim excess. Hot glue a button to frame over each wire end. Hot glue frame to photo.

## 25 Postcard Frame
*(shown on page 113)*

You will need spray adhesive, white cardstock, craft knife, cutting mat, black fine-point permanent pen, 5" x 7" photograph, and a 5" x 7" frame.

*Use adhesive in a well-ventilated area.* For mat, make a color photocopy of design on page 174; cut out. Adhere mat to cardstock; cut out. Use craft knife to cut out opening. Use pen to darken inner edges of mat where white cardstock shows. Insert mat, then photo in frame.

Pumpkin Seed Favors, page 154

Pumpkin Bread, page 110

*tip*

To make a Fleece Table Runner like the one on page 119, determine how wide you would like your table runner, then cut a piece of striped fleece this width and long enough to drape over the ends of your table. Make cuts along each end for fringe.

## 1 Mr. and Mrs. Snowman
*(shown on page 119)*

You will need two 1-gallon plastic bottles (we used vinegar bottles), craft knife and cutting mat, $1/2$ yd white and $1/4$ yd purple 60"w fleece, scrap of orange fleece, hot glue gun, tracing paper, pink acrylic paint, paintbrush, four $5/8$" dia. black shank buttons with shanks removed for eyes, $3/8$" dia. black buttons for mouth, assorted ribbons, $1 1/8$" dia. flower button, twigs for hair, spray adhesive, and mica flakes.

*Use caution when working with glue gun. Use adhesive in a well-ventilated area.*

1. Mark around each bottle $7 1/2$" from bottom. Use craft knife to cut top from bottle; discard top.
2. Cut a $20 1/2$" x $16 1/2$" piece from white fleece. Overlapping fleece edges at back and overlapping bottom edge of bottle by $1 1/2$", hot glue fleece around bottle. Fold and glue excess fleece at top to inside of bottle.
3. For nose, trace pattern, page 173, onto tracing paper; cut out. Using pattern, cut nose from orange fleece. Roll nose into a cone; hot glue to secure. Fold $1/4$" of open end of nose to the inside.
4. Dry brush cheeks on front of bottle with pink paint. Hot glue buttons and nose to bottle for face.
5. For lady, tie several ribbon lengths into a bow. Hot glue to top edge of bottle. Hot glue flower button to center of bow. For scarf on man, cut an 8" x 45" piece from purple fleece. For fringe, make 3" long cuts, $1/2$" apart, along each end. Wrap scarf around bottom edge of bottle, knotting ends at one side.
6. Apply adhesive to twigs. Sprinkle mica flakes onto twigs; shake off excess and allow to dry. Arrange twigs in bottles.

## 2 Fleece Scarves
*(shown on page 120)*

To make 10 scarves, you will need $2 1/2$ yds of 60"w fleece and a rotary cutter and cutting mat.

For each scarf, cut a 9" x 60" strip from fleece; trim selvages. For fringe, make 5" long cuts, $3/4$" apart, along each end.

## 3 Songbook
*(shown on page 121)*

You will need white scrapbook paper, decorative-edged craft scissors, 12" x 12" blue cardstock, $1/4$" dia. hole punch, spray adhesive, and assorted ribbons.

*Use adhesive in a well-ventilated area.*

1. Make a color photocopy on white paper of design on page 175; use craft scissors to trim $1/4$" from design.
2. For front cover, cut a $5 1/4$"w x 12"h strip from cardstock. For top edge, fold $1 3/4$" of one end of strip to the back. Use spray adhesive to glue design to cover. For back cover, cut a $5 1/4$"w x $10 1/4$"h strip from cardstock.
3. For inside pages, print or write song lyrics on $4 1/4$"w x $9 1/2$"h strips of white paper.
4. Aligning top edges of inside pages with top edge of back cover, stack pages on cover. Place fold of front cover over top edge of inside pages and back cover. Punch two holes, $3/4$" apart and $1/2$" from top edge, in center of covers and pages.
5. Thread ribbons through holes in songbook and tie into a bow at front.

## 4 Snow-Lined Mugs
*(shown on page 119)*

To make 10 mugs, you will need 10 Design-A-Mug kits, spray adhesive, mica flakes, tacky glue, and $1/4$ yd of 60"w fleece.

*Use adhesive in a well-ventilated area.*

1. Remove white insert from each mug. Spray adhesive inside clear mug. Sprinkle mica flakes over adhesive; allow to dry.
2. Apply tacky glue under rim of insert. Replace insert in mug, pressing firmly to seal.
3. For scarf, cut a $1 1/4$" x 19" strip from fleece. For fringe, make 1" long cuts, $1/4$" apart, along each end of strip. Wrap scarf around mug; knot ends around handle.

## 5 Cabled Pillow
*(shown on page 135)*

Finished Size: 14" square (36 cm)

*Read Knit and Crochet Basics, pages 168 – 169, before beginning Pillow.*

### MATERIALS

Worsted Weight Yarn:
  6½ ounces, 445 yards (180 grams, 407 meters)
straight knitting needles, size 8 (5.00 mm) **or** size needed for gauge
14" square (36 cm) pillow form
cable needle
yarn needle

**GAUGE:** In pattern, 29 sts = 4⅜" (11 cm); 16 rows = 2¼" (6 cm)
      In Stockinette Stitch, 18 sts and 24 rows = 4" (10 cm)
**Gauge Swatch:** 4" square (10 cm)
Cast on 18 sts **loosely**.
Work in Stockinette Stitch for 23 rows.
Bind off all sts in pattern.

### STITCH GUIDE
**CABLE 4 BACK (abbreviated C4B)**
  (uses next 4 sts)
Slip next 2 sts onto cable needle and hold in **back** of work, K2 from left needle, K2 from cable needle.

**CABLE 4 FRONT (abbreviated C4F)**
  (uses next 4 sts)
Slip next 2 sts onto cable needle and hold in **front** of work, K2 from left needle, K2 from cable needle.

**TWIST 3 BACK (abbreviated T3B)**
  (uses next 3 sts)
Slip next st onto cable needle and hold in **back** of work, K2 from left needle, P1 from cable needle.

**TWIST 3 FRONT (abbreviated T3F)**
  (uses next 3 sts)
Slip next 2 sts onto cable needle and hold in **front** of work, P1 from left needle, K2 from cable needle.

**TWIST 4 BACK (abbreviated T4B)**
  (uses next 4 sts)
Slip next 2 sts onto cable needle and hold in **back** of work, K2 from left needle, P2 from cable needle.

**TWIST 4 FRONT (abbreviated T4F)**
  (uses next 4 sts)
Slip next 2 sts onto cable needle and hold in **front** of work, P2 from left needle, K2 from cable needle.

## FRONT
Cast on 90 sts **loosely**.

**Row 1** (Right side): K1, P6, K4, (P4, K4) twice, ★ P8, K4, (P4, K4) twice; repeat from ★ once **more**, P6, K1.
**Row 2:** P1, K6, P4, (K4, P4) twice, ★ K8, P4, (K4, P4) twice; repeat from ★ once **more**, K6, P1.
**Row 3:** K1, P6, C4B, (P4, C4B) twice, ★ P8, C4B, (P4, C4B) twice; repeat from ★ once **more**, P6, K1.
**Row 4:** P1, K6, P4, (K4, P4) twice, ★ K8, P4, (K4, P4) twice; repeat from ★ once **more**, K6, P1.
**Row 5:** K1, P5, T3B, (T4F, T4B) twice, T3F, ★ P6, T3B, (T4F, T4B) twice, T3F; repeat from ★ once **more**, P5, K1.
**Row 6:** P1, K5, P2, K3, P4, K4, P4, K3, P2, ★ K6, P2, K3, P4, K4, P4, K3, P2; repeat from ★ once **more**, K5, P1.
**Row 7:** K1, P4, ★ T3B, P3, C4F, P4, C4B, P3, T3F, P4; repeat from ★ 2 times **more**, K1.
**Row 8:** P1, K4, ★ P2, K4, (P4, K4) twice, P2, K4; repeat from ★ 2 times **more**, P1.
**Row 9:** K1, P4, ★ K2, P3, T3B, T4F, T4B, T3F, P3, K2, P4; repeat from ★ 2 times **more**, K1.
**Row 10:** P1, K4, ★ (P2, K3) twice, P4, (K3, P2) twice, K4; repeat from ★ 2 times **more**, P1.
**Row 11:** K1, P4, ★ (K2, P3) twice, C4B, (P3, K2) twice, P4; repeat from ★ 2 times **more**, K1.
**Row 12:** P1, K4, ★ (P2, K3) twice, P4, (K3, P2) twice, K4; repeat from ★ 2 times **more**, P1.
**Row 13:** K1, P4, ★ K2, P3, T3F, T4B, T4F, T3B, P3, K2, P4; repeat from ★ 2 times **more**, K1.
**Row 14:** P1, K4, ★ P2, K4, (P4, K4) twice, P2, K4; repeat from ★ 2 times **more**, P1.
**Row 15:** K1, P4, ★ T3F, P3, C4F, P4, C4B, P3, T3B, P4; repeat from ★ 2 times **more**, K1.
**Row 16:** P1, K5, P2, K3, P4, K4, P4, K3, P2, ★ K6, P2, K3, P4, K4, P4, K3, P2; repeat from ★ once **more**, K5, P1.
**Row 17:** K1, P5, T3F, (T4B, T4F) twice, T3B, ★ P6, T3F, (T4B, T4F) twice, T3B; repeat from ★ once **more**, P5, K1.
Repeat Rows 2-17 for pattern until piece measures approximately 13" (33 cm) from cast on edge, ending by working a **wrong** side row.
Bind off all sts in **purl**.

## BACK
Work same as Front.

## ASSEMBLY
With **wrong** sides of Front and Back together, sew pieces together inserting pillow form before closing.

## 6 Trinity Pillow
*(shown on page 135)*

Finished Size: 14" square (36 cm)

*Read Knit and Crochet Basics, pages 168 – 169, before beginning Pillow.*

### MATERIALS

Worsted Weight Yarn:
  6 ounces, 410 yards (170 grams, 375 meters)
straight knitting needles, size 8 (5.00 mm) **or** size needed for gauge
14" square (36 cm) pillow form
yarn needle

**GAUGE:** In pattern, 16 sts and 17 rows = 2½" (6.4 cm)
**Gauge Swatch:** 2¾"w x 2½"h (7 cm x 6.4 cm)
Cast on 18 sts **loosely**.
Work same as Front for 16 rows.
Bind off all sts in **purl**.

## FRONT
Cast on 82 sts **loosely**.
**Row 1** (Right side): Purl across.
**Row 2:** K1, ★ (K, P, K) all in next st, P3 tog (**Fig. 8, page 169**); repeat from ★ across to last st, K1.
**Row 3:** Purl across.
**Row 4:** K1, ★ P3 tog, (K, P, K) all in next st; repeat from ★ across to last st, K1.
**Row 5:** Purl across.
Repeat Rows 2-5 for pattern until piece measures approximately 13" (33 cm) from cast on edge, ending by working a **wrong** side row.
Bind off all sts in **purl**.

## BACK
Work same as Front.

## ASSEMBLY
With **wrong** sides of Front and Back together, sew pieces together inserting pillow form before closing.

**tip** Place cedar chips inside doggie's bed to add a fresh scent.

## 7 Faux Fur Throw
*(shown on page 134)*

You will need 1⁷/₈ yds each of 60"w red and black buffalo plaid wool and 60"w brown faux fur fabric.

Cut a 51" x 64" piece each from wool and fur fabric. Matching right sides and leaving an opening for turning, use a ¹/₂" seam allowance to sew pieces together. Clip corners, turn right side out, and press; slip stitch opening closed.

## 8 Horse Collar Wreath
*(shown on page 126)*

You will need a hot glue gun, floral wire, wire cutters, artificial greenery and berries, horse collar, 3 yd length of braided straw rope, 6¹/₄ yd length of red braided nylon rope, two 3³/₄" dia. gold sleigh bells, jute twine, transfer paper, 5¹/₂" x 13¹/₂" cream crackled metal plaque, red and green paint pens, and a black medium-point permanent pen.

*Use caution when working with glue gun.*
1. Hot gluing in spots as needed, use wire to attach greenery and berries to top of collar.
2. Securing at center with wire, arrange straw rope into a bow; use wire to attach bow to top of collar. Repeat with nylon rope. Apply hot glue to straw rope ends and knot nylon rope ends to prevent fraying. Tie bells to top of collar with twine.
3. Use a photocopier to enlarge pattern, page 175, to 176%; transfer onto plaque. Paint design with paint pens and allow to dry. Outline design with black pen. Hot glue plaque to collar. Hot glue greenery and berries to collar below plaque.

## 9 Tray Entryway Decoration
*(shown on page 127)*

You will need sandpaper, spray primer, an oval serving tray (ours is wooden with a metal frame), white spray paint, stencil adhesive, stencils for desired saying and designs, stencil brush, moss green acrylic paint, matte clear acrylic spray sealer, artificial floral swag, floral wire, and wire cutters.

*Use spray primer, paint, and sealer in a well-ventilated area. Allow primer, paint, and sealer to dry after each application.*

Sand, then prime tray. Paint entire tray white. Turn tray over, and following adhesive manufacturer's instructions, arrange and adhere stencils on back of tray. Use stencil brush to stencil saying and designs on tray with moss green paint. Remove stencils and apply sealer to entire tray. Attach swag to top of tray with wire.

## 10 Boxwood Monogram
*(shown on page 129)*

You will need a 2" thick green floral foam sheet, serrated knife, hardware cloth, floral wire, wire cutters, and boxwood clippings or artifical boxwood picks.

Print desired letter from computer. Use a photocopier to enlarge letter to desired size; cut out. Draw around letter on foam; cut out with serrated knife. Securing cloth with floral wire, cover foam letter with hardware cloth. Use floral wire to make hanger(s) on back of letter. Covering sides and front of letter, insert clippings or picks in foam.

## 11 Jar Lantern
*(shown on page 132)*

You will need artificial cranberries and key limes, plastic greenery, a 5¹/₄" square x 7"h glass cracker jar with metal lid, two 16-ounce bottles of clear lamp and candle oil, hammer and awl, 2"l x ³/₄" dia. bottle candle converter with fiberglass wick, and a flat-head screwdriver.

*Never leave burning lantern unattended.*
Arrange berries, limes, and greenery in jar. Fill jar with oil. Use hammer and awl to punch a hole in center of lid. Adjust wick in converter so that top of wick is ¹/₈" above top edge of converter. Replace lid on jar, and using screwdriver to enlarge hole as needed, insert converter into hole in lid. Allow wick to fully absorb oil before lighting. Trim wick if necessary to adjust flame.

## 12 Hurricane Lanterns
*(shown on page 137)*

You will need spray primer; assorted colors of spray paint; 36"l x ⁵/₈" dia. wooden dowels; tuna cans; clear acrylic spray sealer; ³/₈" dia. round foam brush and white acrylic paint (optional); clear glass hurricane shades to fit in cans; hammer and nail; drill with ³/₃₂" dia. bit; screwdriver; #10 x ³/₄" screws; floral wire; wire cutters; assorted ribbons, ornaments, silk flowers, and greenery; and candles to fit in cans.

*Use spray primer, paint, and sealer in a well-ventilated area. Allow primer, paint, and sealer to dry after each application. Never leave burning candles unattended.*

1. For each lantern, prime, then paint a dowel and can as desired. Apply sealer. Use foam brush to paint white dots on shade if desired.
2. Use hammer and nail to punch a hole in center bottom of can. Drill a pilot hole in center of one end of dowel. Aligning holes, drive screw through can and dowel.
3. Tie or wire ribbons, ornaments, flowers, and greenery to dowel.
4. Place candle, then shade in can.

## 13 Dog Sweater
*(shown on page 141)*

*Read Knit and Crochet Basics, pages 168 – 169, before beginning Sweater.*

| Size: | Sm | Med | Lg | X-Lg |
|---|---|---|---|---|
| **Finished Measurement:** (from neck to base of tail) | 12" | 14" | 16" | 18" |
| | (31 cm | 36 cm | 41 cm | 46 ) cm |

**Size Note:** Instructions are written for size Small, with sizes Medium, Large, and X-Large in braces { }. Instructions will be easier to read if you circle all the numbers pertaining to your dog's size. If only one number is given, it applies to all sizes.

## MATERIALS

Worsted Weight Yarn:
3{4-5-6} ounces,
90{110-140-170} grams,
[170{225-285-340} yards,
155 {206-261-311} meters]
straight knitting needles, size 7
(4.50 mm) **or** size needed for gauge
stitch holder
two markers
two ³/₄" dia. buttons
yarn needle

**GAUGE:** In pattern, 20 sts and 26 rows = 4" (10 cm)

## BODY

Cast on 40{44-52-56} sts.
**Row 1:** Knit across.
**Rows 2-7:** K1, increase (**Figs. 9a & 9b, page 169**), knit across to last 2 sts, increase, K1: 52{56-64-68} sts.
**Row 8** (Right side): K6, place marker, knit across to last 6 sts, place marker, K6.
**Note:** Loop a short piece of yarn around any stitch to mark Row 8 as **right** side.
**Rows 9 and 10:** Knit across to first marker, (P2, K2) across to next marker, knit across.
**Rows 11 and 12:** Knit across to first marker, (K2, P2) across to next marker, knit across.
Repeat Rows 9-12 for pattern until Body measures approximately 11{13-15-17}"/28{33-38-43} cm from cast on edge, ending by working a **wrong** side row.

## NECK SHAPING

**Note:** Both sides of the Neck are worked at the same time, using separate yarn for each side.
**Row 1:** Work across 18{18-20-22} sts, slip next 16{20-24-24} sts onto st holder; with second yarn, work across: 18{18-20-22} sts **each** side.
**Row 2** (Decrease row): Work across to within 2 sts of Neck edge, K2 tog (**Fig. 5, page 169**); with second yarn, slip 1 as if to **knit**, K1, PSSO (**Fig. 4, page 169**), work across: 17{17-19-21} sts **each** side.
**Rows 3 and 4:** Repeat Row 2: 15{15-17-19} sts **each** side.
Continue to decrease one stitch at **each** neck edge, every other row, 3{3-4-5} times: 12{12-13-14} sts **each** side.

Work even until Sweater measures approximately 14{16¹/₂-18¹/₂-21}"/35.5{42-47-53.5} cm from cast on edge, ending by working a **wrong** side row.
Bind off all sts.

## FINISHING
### NECKBAND

With **right** side facing, pick up 18{22-22-24} sts along right Neck edge (**Fig. 10, page 169**), slip 16{20-24-24} sts from st holder onto empty needle and knit across, pick up 18{22-22-24} sts along left Neck edge: 52{64-68-72} sts.
Knit 8 rows.
Bind off all sts in knit.

### BAND

With **right** side facing and beginning 5¹/₂{6¹/₂-7¹/₂-8¹/₂}"/14{16.5-19-21.5}cm down from left bound off edge, pick up 10 sts evenly spaced across 2".
Knit every row until Sweater fits snugly around dog's chest.
**Next Row** (Buttonhole row): K2, YO (buttonhole) (**Fig. 2, page 169**), K2 tog, K2, K2 tog, YO (buttonhole), K2.
Knit 3 rows.
Bind off all sts in **knit**.
Sew end of right Neck to end of left Neck.
Weave in yarn ends.
Sew buttons to Body opposite band.

**Design by Evie Rosen**

## 14 Doggie Duvet
*(shown on page 141)*

You will need 1³/₄ yds of 60"w plaid fleece, rotary cutter and cutting mat, and a 28" square pillow form.

For duvet, cut a 33" x 61" piece from fleece. Matching right sides, use a ¹/₂" seam allowance to sew ends together to form a tube; turn right side out. Press duvet flat with seam at center back. For end ties, make a 7¹/₂" long cut into each pressed edge. Cutting through both layers of fleece, use rotary cutter to cut 7¹/₂" long ties, 1¹/₄" apart, along open edges. Slip duvet over pillow form with seam at center back. Double-knot ties in pairs across open sides of duvet.

*tip*

To prevent sticky fingers when spraying Faux Snowballs with adhesive, poke a piece of wire or a craft stick into foam ball to create a handle before spraying.

## 15 Snowman Banner
*(shown on page 142)*

You will need $^5/_8$ yd white, $^5/_8$ yd purple, and $^1/_4$ yd plaid 60"w fleece; scraps of pink, orange, and black fleece or felt; $^7/_8$"w fusible web tape; paper-backed fusible web; hot glue gun; 11 black buttons; two silk flowers removed from stems; and a 19"l x $^1/_2$" dia. wooden dowel.

*Use caution when working with glue gun.*

1. For banner, cut a 19" x 56" piece from white fleece. Matching ends, fold fleece in half; mark fold, then unfold fleece. Fuse web tape along wrong side of fleece on one end and both sides, stopping 2" from fold. Refold fleece and fuse edges together.
2. For hat, cut a 19" square from purple fleece. For fringe, make $4^1/_2$" long cuts, 1" apart, along one edge of hat. Cut a 6" x 19" piece of fusible web; fuse to wrong side along opposite edge. Overlapping folded edge of white fleece by 6", fuse hat to banner.
3. For hat cuff, cut a 10" x 25" strip each from purple fleece and fusible web; fuse web to wrong side of fleece. Matching wrong sides, fold long edges to center of strip; fuse in place. Wrapping ends to back, hot glue cuff across banner $1^3/_4$" below folded edge.
4. For eyes, cut two $2^1/_4$" squares with wavy edges from black fleece or felt. Cut two $3^1/_4$" dia. circles from pink fleece or felt for cheeks. Cut a 7"-long nose from orange fleece or felt. Hot glue eyes, cheeks, and nose to center of banner. Hot glue buttons to banner for mouth.
5. For scarf, cut a $5^1/_4$" x 22" piece each from fusible web and plaid fleece; fuse web to wrong side of fleece. Remove paper backing and, wrapping ends to back, fuse scarf to bottom of banner. Cut a $5^1/_4$" x 36" strip from plaid fleece. For fringe, make 4" long cuts, $^3/_4$" apart, at ends of strip. Knot strip at center; hot glue knot to scarf on banner.

6. Hot glue flowers to hat cuff. To stabilize banner, insert dowel in opening at folded edge of banner. Cut a 1" x 18" strip from purple fleece. Gathering fringed end of hat, tightly knot strip around hat; hot glue at back to secure. For hanging loop, knot strip ends together 1" from first knot.

## 16 Snowman Bucket
*(shown on page 143)*

You will need paper-backed fusible web; $^5/_8$ yd white and $^1/_4$ yd striped 60"w fleece; scraps of pink, orange, and black fleece or felt; hot glue gun; and a $10^1/_2$"h x 11" dia. galvanized bucket.

*Use caution when working with glue gun.*

1. For cover, cut one $34^1/_4$" x $9^5/_8$" piece from fusible web and two $34^1/_4$" x $9^5/_8$" pieces from white fleece. Layer and fuse fleece pieces together.
2. For eyes, cut two $1^5/_8$" squares with wavy edges from black fleece or felt. Cut two $3^1/_4$" dia. circles from pink fleece or felt for cheeks. Cut a 5"-long nose from orange fleece or felt. Hot glue eyes, cheeks, and nose to center of cover.
3. Trimming and overlapping fleece at back as necessary, hot glue cover around bucket.
4. For scarf, cut a $7^1/_2$" x 56" piece from striped fleece. For fringe, make 4" long cuts, $^3/_4$" apart, along each end. Wrap scarf around bottom edge of bucket, knotting ends at one side.

## 17 Faux Snowballs
*(shown on page 143)*

You will need spray adhesive, 3" dia. foam balls, low-loft batting, mica flakes, and a large plastic zip-top bag.

*Use adhesive in a well-ventilated area. If children will be playing with snowballs, leave off the mica flakes.* Spray foam balls with adhesive. Tear pieces from batting; cover balls with torn pieces. Pour mica flakes into zip-top bag. Apply spray adhesive to covered balls and drop them in bag. Seal bag and shake to cover balls with mica flakes.

## 18 Friendly Snow Fellow Chairback Cover
*(shown on page 143)*

You will need paper-backed fusible web; $^7/_8$ yd white and $^1/_4$ yd polka-dot 60"w fleece; scraps of pink, orange, and black fleece or felt; 2" x 4" hook-and-loop fastener; assorted-size black buttons; hot glue gun; and a wooden folding chair.

*Use caution when working with glue gun. Our chairback cover was made for a 17"w x 15$^1/_2$"h chair back. You may need to adjust the size of your cover to fit your chair.*

1. For chairback cover, cut one 15" x 29" piece from fusible web and two 15" x 29" pieces from white fleece. Layer and fuse fleece pieces together.
2. From polka-dot fleece, cut a 4" x 35$^1/_2$" strip for front scarf and a 4" x 34" strip for back scarf. For fringe, make 3$^1/_2$" long cuts, $^3/_4$" apart, along one end of each strip. Sew one half of fastener to right side of unfringed end of back scarf piece; sew remaining half of fastener to wrong side of unfringed end of front scarf piece.
3. Cut two 4" x 15" strips from fusible web. Matching edges, fuse a web strip along each end on right side of chairback cover; remove paper backing. Referring to **Fig. 1** and aligning unfringed end with edge of chairback cover, fuse back scarf piece to one end of chairback cover. With 6" of unfringed end extended past edge of chairback cover, fuse front scarf piece along remaining end of chairback cover. Matching ends and wrong sides, fold chairback cover in half.

**Fig. 1**

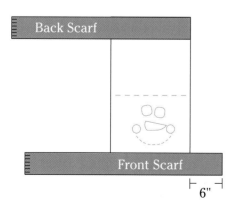

4. For eyes, cut two 1$^5/_8$" squares with wavy edges from black fleece or felt. Cut two 3$^1/_4$" dia. circles from pink fleece or felt for cheeks. Cut a 5"-long nose from orange fleece or felt. Hot glue eyes, cheeks, and nose to center of chairback cover front. Hot glue buttons to cover for mouth.
5. Place cover over chair back. Wrapping front scarf piece around back leg of chair, fasten hook-and-loop fastener. Knot fringed scarf ends together around remaining back leg.

## 19 Pillar Candles
*(shown on page 144)*

You will need color photocopies of cards, decorative-edged craft scissors (optional), paraffin wax, 3" dia. pillar candles, and paintbrushes.

*Use caution when working with hot wax. Never leave burning candles unattended.*
Using craft scissors if desired, cut out photocopied designs. Melt paraffin in a double boiler. For each candle, brush paraffin on candle where you would like your design; press design onto candle over paraffin. Brush a light coat of paraffin over design; allow to dry.

## 20 Brown Bag Luminaries
*(shown on page 144)*

You will need lunch-size brown paper bags, gold spray paint, $^1/_4$" dia. hole punch, $^1/_4$"w green ribbon, prepasted wallpaper pieces, sand, and tea light candles.

*Use spray paint in a well-ventilated area. Never leave burning candles unattended.*

1. For each luminaria, fold top of bag 1$^1/_4$" to outside twice. Lightly spray bag with gold paint; allow to dry.
2. Punch two holes, $^1/_2$" apart, in center of folded section on front of bag. Knot a length of ribbon through holes.

3. Follow manufacturer's instructions to adhere wallpaper piece to front of bag.
4. Fill 1" of bottom of bag with sand; secure candle in sand at center of bag.

## 21 Memory Tree
*(shown on page 145)*

You will need decorative-edged craft scissors, photographs, craft glue, black cardstock, paper-backed fusible vinyl, $^1/_4$" dia. hole punch, $^3/_8$"w green ribbon, silver metallic thread, assorted-size green glass ball ornaments, and a black ornament tree.

For each photo ornament, use craft scissors to trim photo as desired. Glue photo to cardstock; cut out $^1/_8$" outside edges of photo. Remove paper backing from vinyl. Place vinyl, adhesive side down, on photo. Smooth with fingers to remove air bubbles. Using paper backing as a pressing cloth, fuse vinyl to photo. Repeat for back of ornament. Trim vinyl even with edges of cardstock. Punch a hole in top of each photo ornament. Use ribbon or thread to tie photo ornaments to tree; tie glass ornaments to tree with ribbon.

## CUTTING A FABRIC CIRCLE

1. Matching right sides, fold fabric square in half from top to bottom and again from left to right.
2. Tie one end of a length of string to a fabric marking pen. Measuring from pen, insert a thumbtack through string at length indicated in project instructions. Insert thumbtack through folded corner of fabric. Holding tack in place and keeping string taut, mark cutting line (**Fig. 1**).

**Fig. 1**

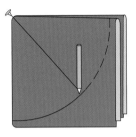

## KNIT AND CROCHET BASICS
### Abbreviations

| | |
|---|---|
| ch(s) | chain(s) |
| cm | centimeter(s) |
| dc | double crochet(s) |
| hdc | half double crochet(s) |
| K | knit |
| mm | millimeter(s) |
| P | purl |
| PSSO | pass slipped stitch over |
| Rnd(s) | Round(s) |
| sc | single crochet(s) |
| sp(s) | space(s) |
| st(s) | stitch(es) |
| tog | together |
| YO | yarn over |

**( )** or **[ ]** – work enclosed instructions as many times as specified by the number immediately following **or** work all enclosed instructions in the stitch or space indicated **or** contains explanatory remarks.

**colon (:)** – the number(s) given after a colon at the end of a row or round denote(s) the number of stitches or spaces you should have on that row or round.

### Gauge

Exact gauge is essential for proper size. Before beginning your project, make the sample swatch given in the individual instructions with the weight of yarn and hook size specified.

After completing the swatch, measure it, counting your stitches and rows or rounds carefully. If your swatch is larger or smaller than specified, make another, changing hook size to get the correct gauge. Keep trying until you find the size hook that will give you the specified gauge.

### Crochet Markers

Markers are used to help distinguish the beginning of each round being worked. Place a 2" (5 cm) scrap of yarn before the first stitch of each round, moving marker after each round is complete.

### Joining with Sc

When instructed to join with sc, begin with a slip knot on hook. Insert hook in stitch or space indicated, YO and pull up a loop, YO and draw through both loops on hook.

| KNITTING NEEDLES | | |
|---|---|---|
| UNITED STATES | ENGLISH U.K. | METRIC (mm) |
| 0 | 13 | 2 |
| 1 | 12 | 2.25 |
| 2 | 11 | 2.75 |
| 3 | 10 | 3.25 |
| 4 | 9 | 3.5 |
| 5 | 8 | 3.75 |
| 6 | 7 | 4 |
| 7 | 6 | 4.5 |
| 8 | 5 | 5 |
| 9 | 4 | 5.5 |
| 10 | 3 | 6 |
| 10½ | 2 | 6.5 |
| 11 | 1 | 8 |
| 13 | 00 | 9 |
| 15 | 000 | 10 |
| 17 | — | 12.75 |

| KNIT TERMINOLOGY | |
|---|---|
| UNITED STATES | INTERNATIONAL |
| gauge = | tension |
| bind off = | cast off |
| yarn over (YO) = | yarn forward (yfwd) **or** yarn around needle (yrn) |

| CROCHET TERMINOLOGY | |
|---|---|
| UNITED STATES | INTERNATIONAL |
| slip stitch (slip st) = | single crochet (sc) |
| single crochet (sc) = | double crochet (dc) |
| half double crochet (hdc) = | half treble crochet (htr) |
| double crochet (dc) = | treble crochet (tr) |
| treble crochet (tr) = | double treble crochet (dtr) |
| double treble crochet (dtr) = | triple treble crochet (ttr) |
| triple treble crochet (tr tr) = | quadruple treble crochet (qtr) |
| skip = | miss |

| ALUMINUM CROCHET HOOKS | |
|---|---|
| UNITED STATES | METRIC (mm) |
| B-1 | 2.25 |
| C-2 | 2.75 |
| D-3 | 3.25 |
| E-4 | 3.5 |
| F-5 | 3.75 |
| G-6 | 4 |
| H-8 | 5 |
| I-9 | 5.5 |
| J-10 | 6 |
| K-10½ | 6.5 |
| N | 9 |
| P | 10 |
| Q | 15 |

| Yarn Weight Symbol & Names | SUPER FINE 1 | FINE 2 | LIGHT 3 | MEDIUM 4 | BULKY 5 | SUPER BULKY 6 |
|---|---|---|---|---|---|---|
| Type of Yarns in Category | Sock, Fingering Baby | Sport, Baby | DK, Light Worsted | Worsted, Afghan, Aran | Chunky, Craft, Rug | Bulky, Roving |
| Advised Hook Size Range | B-1 to E-4 | E-4 to 7 | 7 to I-9 | I-9 to K-10.5 | K-10.5 to M-13 | M-13 and larger |
| Advised Needle Size Range | 1-3 | 3-5 | 5-7 | 7-9 | 9-11 | 11 and larger |

## Knit Markers
**Fig. 1**

Place markers as instructed. When you reach a marker on a row, slip it from the left needle to the right needle (**Fig. 1**); remove it when no longer needed.

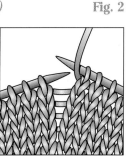

## Yarn Over (YO)
**Fig. 2**

Bring the yarn forward between the needles, then back over the top of the right needle, so that it is now in position to knit the next stitch (**Fig. 2**).

## Purl 2 Together (P2 Tog)
**Fig. 3**

Insert the right needle into the front of the first two stitches on the left needle as if to purl, then purl them together as if they were one stitch (**Fig. 3**).

## Slip 1, Knit 1, Pass Slipped Stitch Over (Slip 1, K1, PSSO)
**Fig. 4**

Slip one stitch as if to knit, then knit the next stitch. With the left needle, bring the slipped stitch over the knit stitch (**Fig. 4**) and off the needle.

## Knit 2 Together (K2 tog)
**Fig. 5**

Insert the right needle into the front of the first two stitches on the left needle as if to knit (**Fig. 5**), then knit them together as if they were one stitch.

## Slip 1, Knit 2 Together, Pass Slipped Stitch Over (Slip 1, K2 tog, PSSO)
**Fig. 6**

Slip one stitch as if to knit, then knit the next two stitches together (**Fig. 5**). With the left needle, bring the slipped stitch over the stitch just made (**Fig. 6**) and off the needle.

## Knit 3 Together (K3 tog)
**Fig. 7**

Insert the right needle into the front of the first three stitches on the left needle as if to knit (**Fig. 7**), then knit them together as if they were one stitch.

## Purl 3 Together (P3 tog)
**Fig. 8**

Insert the right needle into the front of the first three stitches on the left needle as if to purl (**Fig. 8**), then purl them together.

## Knit Increases
**Fig. 9a**

To make a knit increase, knit the next stitch but do not slip the old stitch off the left needle (**Fig. 9a**). Insert the right needle into the back loop of the same stitch (**Fig. 9b**) and knit it, then slip the old stitch off the left needle.

**Fig. 9b**

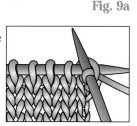
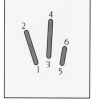

To increase evenly across a row, add one to the number of increases required and divide that number into the number of stitches on the needle. Subtract one from the result and the new number is the appropriate number of stitches to be worked between each increase. Adjust the number as needed. Sometimes it's necessary to work more or less stitches between increases to arrive at the correct total number of stitches.

## Picking Up Stitches
**Fig. 10**

Insert the needle from the front to the back under two strands at the edge of the worked piece (**Fig. 10**). Wrap the yarn around the needle as if to knit, then bring the needle with the yarn back through the stitch to the right side, resulting in a stitch on the needle. Repeat this along the edge, picking up the required number of stitches. A crochet hook may be helpful to pull yarn through.

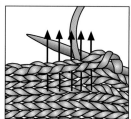

## EMBROIDERY

Follow the stitch diagrams to bring the needle up at odd numbers and down at even numbers.

### Blanket Stitch     Running Stitch

### Straight Stitch     Whipstitch

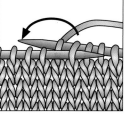

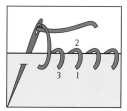

Gift Jars, page 146

Hanging Lantern,
page 151

"Happy Fall" Scrapbook Page,
page 160

Gift Bags, page 150

*Sassy Strawberry Sugar*
*Stir 2 teaspoons flavored sugar*
*Into 6 ounces of iced tea*

*Cheery Cherry Sugar*
*Stir 2 teaspoons flavored sugar*
*Into 6 ounces of iced tea*

*Luscious Lemon Sugar*
*Stir 2 teaspoons flavored sugar*
*Into 6 ounces of iced tea*

# VACATION KEEPSAKES

Vacation Keepsake Valise, page 153

Water Gun Bin, page 153

The best of times

Live life to the fullest.

Wander

Discover

Favorite places

Family Fun

Play hard

WATER GUNS

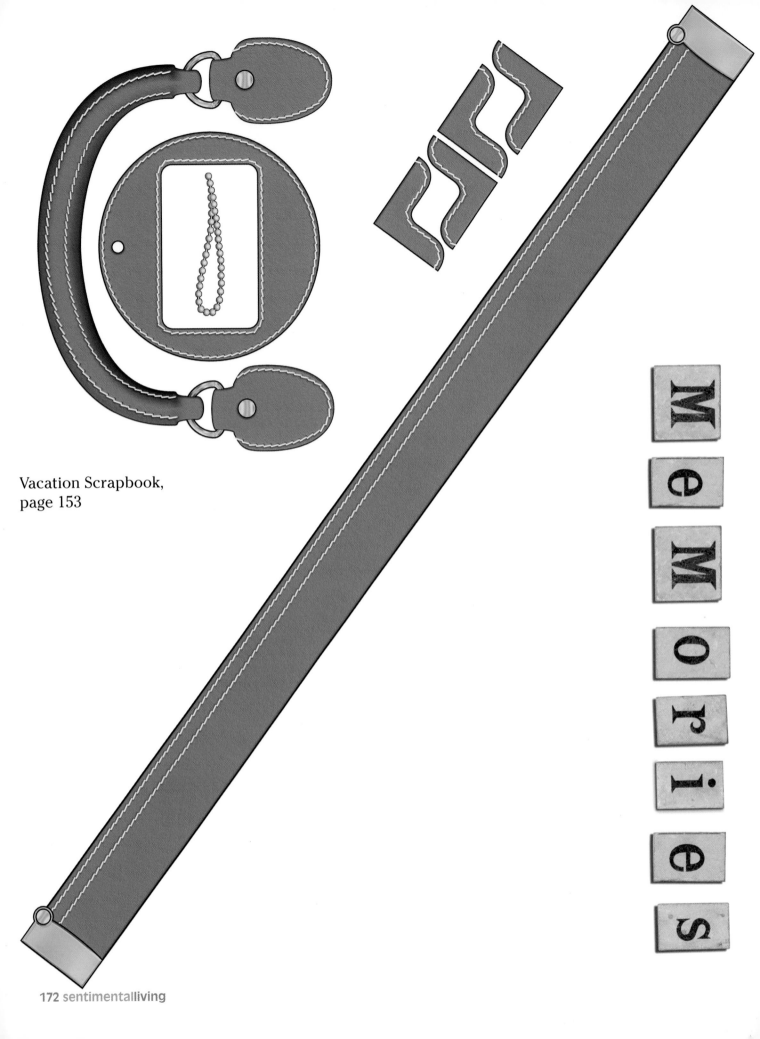

Vacation Scrapbook,
page 153

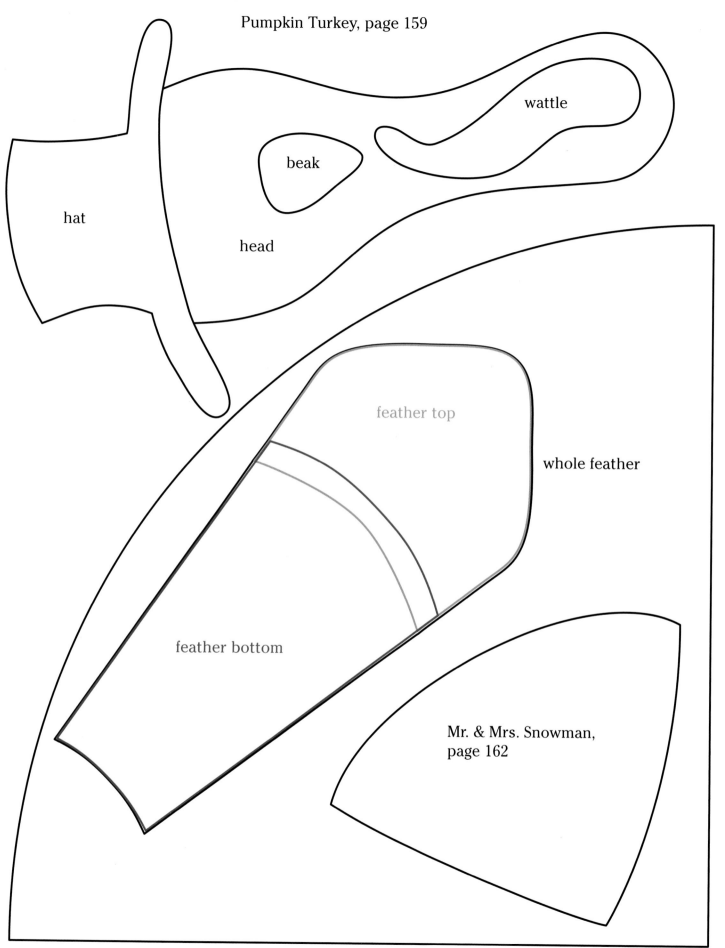

Pumpkin Turkey, page 159

wattle

beak

hat

head

feather top

whole feather

feather bottom

Mr. & Mrs. Snowman,
page 162

Gift Cones, page 155

Candy Corn Bottom

Candy Corn
Pillows,
page 157

Place on fold.

Candy Corn Top

Candy Corn Middle    Place on fold.

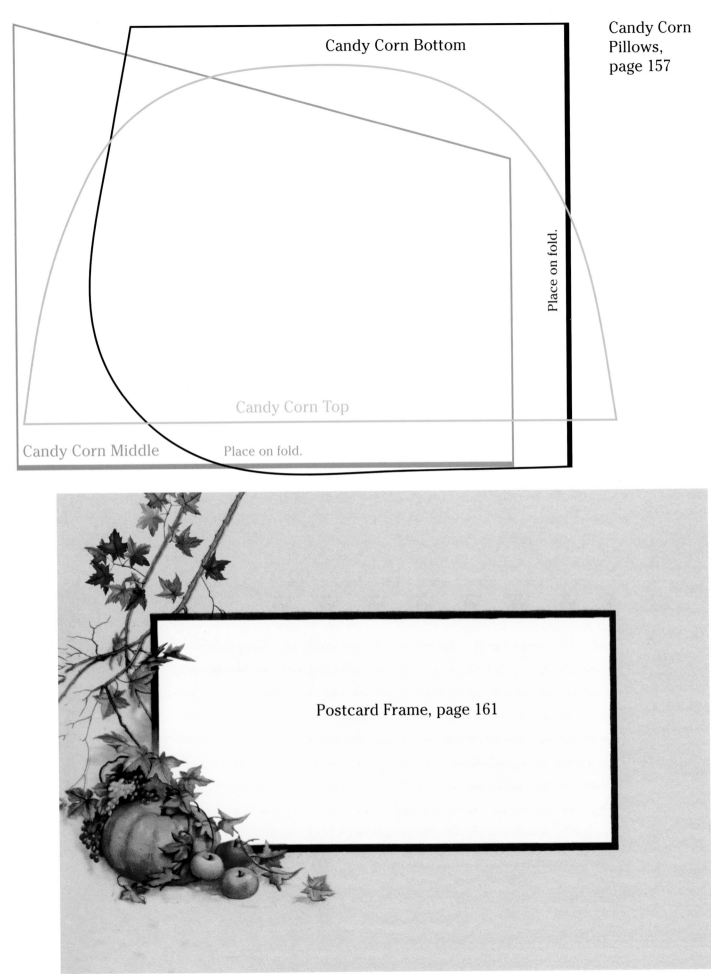

Postcard Frame, page 161

Songbook, page 162

Horse Collar Wreath, page 164

## My Songbook

Gift Boxes, page 130

# From My Heart... A Special Thank You...

Anyone who knows me knows how much I love home and the chance to share my heart with the reader. There are a few very special people who caught my vision and really understood Sentimental Living. The opportunity of creating this book has been an exciting pleasure and to these very special friends I wish to extend very many thanks.

Twenty-something years ago I was fortunate enough to begin a friendship with Sandra Case of Leisure Arts. She understood my love for family, friends, home, and my faith. I will be forever grateful for the friendship, trust, and guidance with which she has blessed me. As an Editor-in-Chief who is enormously talented, she understood my vision of this book. Without her it would not exist, and her guidance on these pages is invaluable. I am truly thankful.

Patti Uhiren is the most creative person I know! As Project Director, she never ceased to amaze me with her talented way of pulling this all together. Her tireless efforts and creative input were invaluable. Patti's never-ending enthusiasm for this project was enormous and her efforts inspired us all.

Mark Mathews is simply the best photographer with whom I've ever worked! Thank you, Mark, for your patience, diligence, and search for perfection. It has been my honor to work with you once again, for *you* will always be my "painter of light."

Thank you to everyone at Leisure Arts, especially multi-talented stylist Christy Meyers, copywriter Susan Johnson, technical writer Christina Kirkendoll, and layout designer Dana Vaughn. To Susan Sullivan, my friend of a lifetime, thank you for your work behind the scenes. For the most wonderful assistance in preparing beautiful presentations of the recipes, my special thanks to Rose Klein.

My special gratitude goes to my terrific sister Cheryl Johnson, who graciously opened up her home and shared the spirit of hospitality that our mother taught us so well. Thank you, Jacob and Christina, for "partying" on the porch with us! And thank you to my friend Mary Morgan who kept me covered with her prayers.

A great big "Thank you" to my husband who put up with my long list of "honey-dos" and honored them. To my sons, Samuel and Mason, thank you for your support when your hard work was needed.

Many thanks to my Aunt Eloise whom I love dearly. And my heartfelt thanks go to the "Steele Magnolias" who have gone before me in extending the spirit of the porch as it spilled onto these pages ... my darling mother, and my strong Southern grandmother who used to *wax* her front porch!

Most Sincerely,

Alda

Alda Ellis

## In Appreciation:

*Thank you to all those who let us step onto their porches:*

*Lange Cheek, Chrissy & Boyd Chitwood, Sandra Cook, Bret & Jennifer Franks, Chuck & Jeanette Heinbockel, Shirley Held, Dennis & Cheryl Johnson, Sharon Mosley, Ellison Poe, Duncan & Nancy Porter, Liz Rice, Sheila Shields, Dan & Jeanne Spencer, Jana Spencer, and Leighton & Doug Weeks*

Many items used in this book, such as the floating candles, silver tray, and canvas chair covers, are available for purchase from Alda's Forever. For more information, visit Alda's Web site at www.SentimentalLiving.com.